Hit & Run
Daring Air Attacks in World War II

Hit & Run

Daring Air Attacks in World War II

Robert Jackson

Pen & Sword

AVIATION

First published in
Great Britain in 2005
By Pen & Sword Aviation
an imprint of Pen and Sword Books Ltd
47 Church Street,
Barnsley
South Yorkshire
S70 2AS
England

ISBN 1-84415-162-X

Typeset in 10/12pt Palatino by Mac Style Ltd, Scarborough, N. Yorkshire
Printed and bound in England by CPI UK

Pen & Sword Books Ltd incorporates the imprints of Pen & Sword
Aviation, Pen & Sword Maritime, Pen & Sword Military, Wharncliffe
Local History, Pen & Sword Select, Pen & Sword Military Classics and
Leo Cooper.

For a complete list of Pen & Sword titles please contact

PEN & SWORD BOOKS LIMITED
47 Church Street, Barnsley, South Yorkshire, S70 2AS, England
E-mail: enquiries@pen-and-sword.co.uk
Website: www.pen-and-sword.co.uk

CONTENTS

CHAPTER ONE

North Sea Battle

I n the early afternoon of 3 September 1939, only a matter of hours after British Prime Minister Neville Chamberlain had announced that Britain was at war with Germany following the latter's invasion of Poland, Royal Air Force Bomber Command flew its first operational sorties of the conflict. Vickers Wellington bombers of Nos 37 and 149 Squadrons, and Handley Page Hampdens of Nos 44, 49 and 83 Squadrons, undertook armed reconnaissances over the North Sea as far as the Bight of Heligoland, and shortly afterwards a lone Bristol Blenheim of No. 139 Squadron took off from RAF Wyton, near Huntingdon, to carry out a photographic reconnaissance of German naval units in the Schillig Roads, off Wilhelmshaven. The crew of the aircraft were Flying Officer A. McPherson, Commander Thompson, Royal Navy, and Corporal V. Arrowsmith.

The Blenheim was the first British aircraft to cross the German frontier in the Second World War, and the photographs it brought back revealed some very worthwhile targets indeed. They showed the battleship *Admiral Scheer* at anchor in the roads, surrounded by several light cruisers and destroyers, and the battlecruisers *Scharnhorst* and *Gneisenau* moored in the River Elbe. As a result of this intelligence, the crews of two Bristol Blenheim squadrons – Nos 107 and 110 – based at RAF Wattisham, Suffolk, were briefed to attack the warships. Within the hour, armourers were loading 500 lb (225 kg) armour-piecing bombs into the Blenheims.

The original briefing had called for a high-level attack, but now came a change of orders: the attack would be made at low level. However armour-piercing bombs dropped at a low altitude would not achieve sufficient velocity to be effective, so the armourers had to start all over again and replace the armour-piercing bombs with ordinary high-explosive 500-pounders, fitted with eleven-second delayed-action fuses. It was the fifth time the bomb loads had been

Bristol Blenheim Mk IV medium bombers taking off on a mission. The wartime censor has obliterated the aircraft's code letters for security reasons. (IWM)

changed in two days, for the squadrons had been standing by for action ever since the news broke that the Germans had invaded Poland.

At last everything was ready. Starting at 16.00, ten Blenheims – five from each squadron – roared one by one down Wattisham's main runway and lifted into an overcast afternoon sky. Five Blenheims of No. 139 Squadron also took off from Wyton, followed by twelve Hampdens of Nos 49 and 83 Squadrons, but bad weather prevented the latter aircraft from finding the target and they eventually returned to their bases.

The Wattisham Blenheims, led by Flight Lieutenant Ken Doran, the most experienced pilot available, sped over the Suffolk coast and set course eastwards, flying in two tight formations of five. As they flew on, Doran noticed that the cloud base was getting steadily lower. The sky was heavily overcast, and dark rainclouds scudded towards the German coast before a strong north-westerly wind. Soon, the Blenheims were flying in a narrow 300 ft (90 metre) gap between the cloud base and a heaving grey sea, the colour of slate. Sometimes, the aircraft were forced to fly as low as 50 ft (15 metres). Already, the pilots were beginning to feel the strain. Flying over the sea at this height was a nerve-racking, exhausting business, and any false move might prove fatal.

Doran peered ahead into the murk, running over the attack plan in his mind. At the briefing they had been told that German 'pocket' battleships – so called because they used every device to save weight without sacrificing gun calibre – were armed with only two types of anti-aircraft weapon, heavy guns and machine guns. The idea was therefore to go in low so that the heavy guns could not be depressed enough to fire on them. To confuse the enemy defences, they were to spread out and attack from three directions.

With the Friesian Islands off to starboard and Heligoland up ahead the Blenheims altered course, turning in towards Wilhelmshaven in driving rain. Then the rain stopped and the cloud base rose to about 500 ft (150 metres), which worried Doran; any further improvement and they might have to contend with enemy fighters.

The Jade Estuary was dead ahead, and suddenly a long, dark shape appeared on the horizon. It took Doran's mind a moment to register that he was looking at the *Admiral Scheer,* and that it was growing larger by the second. On his orders, the two Blenheims on the outside of the 110 Squadron formation, in the lead, broke to left and right, shooting up into the clouds while the other three continued on towards the warship. The German gunners, possibly mistaking the Blenheims for Junkers Ju 88s, which from certain angles looked very similar, held their fire.

Doran pulled back the control column as his observer pressed the bomb release. The two 500-pounders dropped away, one punching into the *Scheer's* superstructure and the other bouncing off the armoured deck into the sea. Neither of them exploded. As the second Blenheim made its attack, it came under heavy fire from the *Scheer's* 20 mm twin-barrelled cannon, armament which the warship was not supposed to have. One of the second aircraft's bombs exploded close to the battleship's side; the other, like Doran's, failed to explode.

The dull sky was suddenly filled with brilliant light as more than a hundred guns on the warships and batteries on shore opened fire. A blazing aircraft dropped out of the clouds and fell in the sea near Mellum Island; it was one of the diversionary Blenheims, caught in the meshes of the flak.

After a brief respite the five Blenheims of No. 107 Squadron attacked in turn, making their approach from the north-west and running through the concentrated fire of every gun in and around the anchorage. The leading Blenheim was hit and exploded; the second, both its engines in flames, crashed into the side of the light cruiser *Emden,* causing some casualties. The third crashed near the shore; the fourth, bracketed by a cluster of heavy shells, cartwheeled across the water and sank. Only the fifth came unscathed through the barrage, dropping its bombs in a beautiful straddle across the *Scheer* before escaping into the overcast. Again, the one bomb that hit the battleship failed to explode.

As the surviving Blenheims flew homewards, their crews were bitterly conscious of the fact that the raid had failed, not because of any lack of courage and determination on their part, but because of useless bombs: old bombs, stored for too long in poor conditions. The price of failure had been five aircraft and fifteen men.

On 14 October 1939, a German U-boat commander named Gunther Prien crept daringly into the big British naval base at Scapa Flow in the Orkneys in *U-47* and sank the battleship *Royal Oak*, causing great loss of life. Two days later, German reconnaissance aircraft, which had been keeping a close watch on the east coast of Scotland, reported that the battlecruiser HMS *Hood* had entered the Firth of Forth and appeared to be making for the naval anchorage at Rosyth.

At 11.00 that morning, nine Junkers 88s of I Gruppe, Kampfgeschwader 30 (I/KG 30), took off from Westerland, on the North Sea island of Sylt, under the command of *Hauptmann* Helmuth Pohle with orders to attack the *Hood* and any other naval units they found at Rosyth. Six weeks after the outbreak of war, German bombers were about to venture into British air space for the first time. There were, however, certain conditions. On the

The British battleship Royal Oak, *sunk in a daring attack by* U-47 *on 14 October 1939 at the Scapa Flow naval base in the Orkey Islands.* (Author's collection)

The Luftwaffe's *'wonder bomber', the Junkers Ju 88, had just entered service at the outbreak of the Second World War. The type went on to serve in every combat role.* (Author's collection)

personal orders of Adolf Hitler, the Ju 88 crews were not to attack the *Hood* if she had already entered harbour. Pohle was not surprised by the directive; at this stage of the war, both the *Luftwaffe* and the Royal Air Force had an unspoken, unwritten agreement that only enemy warships were to be attacked, and bombs were not to be dropped if there was a danger of causing civilian casualties.

The prototype Ju 88 had flown for the first time on 21 December 1936, powered by two 1,000 hp DB 600A in-line engines; the second prototype was essentially similar, except that it was fitted with Jumo 211A radials, the engines that were mostly to power the aircraft throughout its career. A pre-series batch of Ju 88A-0s was completed during the summer of 1939, the first production Ju 88A-1s being delivered to a test unit, *Erprobungskommando* 88. In August 1939 this unit was redesignated I/KG 25, and soon afterwards it became I/KG 30, whose task was to pioneer the new dive-bomber into operational service. Normally based at Greifswald, the *Gruppe* had been deployed forward to Sylt to reduce the distance that had to be flown to the target.

Seventy-five minutes after take-off, Pohle's Ju 88s were flying in loose battle formation up the Firth of Forth. German Intelligence had indicated that the RAF had only a handful of obsolescent Gloster Gladiator biplane fighters in Scotland, so the German crews thought they had little to fear from fighter attack. In fact, Intelligence was wrong. Fighter Command had two Spitfire squadrons, Nos 602 and 603, based at Turnhouse near Edinburgh; both units had exchanged their Gloster Gladiators for Spitfires in August. Also, that very morning, the Hurricanes of No. 607 Squadron had flown into Drem on the southern bank of the Firth.

Pohle's formation droned on. From 13,000 ft (4,000 metres), the crews could see the sprawling, smoke-shrouded complex of Edinburgh, then the spidery structure of the Forth Bridge, beneath their wings. And there, dead ahead on the north bank, was Rosyth.

The first ship Pohle saw on the harbour was the *Hood*, dwarfing the lesser warships that clustered around her. She presented a beautiful target. She lay in forbidden territory, but there were several other cruisers and destroyers anchored in the Firth and Pohle selected a target, pushing the Junkers over into a dive. The flak was coming up thick and fast, rocking the aircraft with near misses as it plummeted towards its objective.

Suddenly, there was a loud bang, and a gale of cold air roared into the cockpit. Pohle glanced up; the transparent hatch in the cockpit roof had gone, taking the upper rearward-firing machine gun with it. He forced his attention back to the target, which now filled his sights. A second later, his bombs fell away and he was rocketing skywards again, crushed down into his seat by the force of gravity. One of the bombs exploded in the water; the other hit the cruiser HMS *Southampton* starboard amidships, smashed through three decks, emerged from the side of the hull and reduced the admiral's barge to matchwood. It failed to explode.

The rear-gunner's voice came over the intercom, warning that enemy fighters were approaching from astern. They were the Spitfires of 602 Squadron. The leading fighter was flown by Flight

Lieutenant Pinkerton. Smoky lines of tracer from the Junkers' rear gun flickered past his wings. Pinkerton fired and saw bullet strikes dance and sparkle on the Junkers' dark green camouflage. There was a flicker of fire from one engine and the bomber started to go down.

The Junkers was losing height steadily. Struggling to keep the aircraft flying on one engine, Pohle sighted a trawler. He said later:

> *I thought it might be Norwegian [Norway was then a neutral country] and turned towards it. I was just able to clear the trawler before ditching the Junkers, although the sea was running at strength 4. The crew of the trawler did not rescue me; instead I was picked up by a Navy destroyer, as well as my badly injured fourth crew member. However, I collapsed on the deck with concussion and facial injuries. My crewman died from his injuries the next day.*

Pohle woke up five days later in Port Edward hospital, Edinburgh. The bodies of the other two crew members, *Unteroffizier* Seydel and *Gefreiter* Schleicher, were recovered from the sea.

A second Ju 88, flown by *Oberleutnant* Storp, was shot down into the sea four miles (6.5 km) north of Port Seton by Red Section of 603

The old battleship HMS Iron Duke *was damaged by a near miss during an attack by Junkers 88s of I/KG 30.* (Author's collection)

Squadron. Storp and two of his crew, *Feldwebel* Köhnke and *Feldwebel* Hielscher, were injured and captured by the crew of the trawler *Dayspring*; the fourth crewman, *Obergefreiter* Krämer, was missing.

The Ju 88s had inflicted only light damage on the cruisers *Southampton* and *Edinburgh* and the destroyer *Mohawk*. The next morning I/KG 30 was in action again, under a new commanding officer, *Hauptmann* Fritz Dönch. This time the target was the naval base at Scapa Flow. But apart from the old depot ship *Iron Duke*, which was damaged by a near miss, they found the nest empty. The British Home Fleet had sought refuge in the Clyde on the west coast of Scotland, out of range of the bombers.

The *Luftwaffe* had failed to gain a victory over the Royal Navy. Before the year was out, however, there was to be a victory of a different kind by the German fighters, and it was to have a major effect on the RAF's bombing policy for a long time to come. On 3 December 1939, 24 Vickers Wellington bombers of Nos 38, 115 and 149 Squadrons took off from their bases at Marham in Norfolk and Mildenhall in Suffolk to attack enemy warships in the Heligoland Bight. Led by Wing Commander R. Kellett, the bombers made rendezvous over Great Yarmouth at 09.40, climbing to 10,000 ft (3,000 metres) over the sea *en route* to their objective. The leading flight of three aircraft sighted Heligoland at 11.26 and the crews made out the outlines of some ships, including two cruisers, lying in the vicinity.

The Wellingtons ran through heavy anti-aircraft fire as they made their approach and two of them were hit, although not seriously. A few moments later the bombers were attacked from astern by Messerschmitt 109s and 110s. These attacks were ineffective and at least one of the fighters was damaged. The Wellingtons bombed from 8,000 ft (2,500 metres), but although some of the bombs fell in the target area no hits were registered on the warships. All the aircraft returned to base.

This operation seemed to justify the belief that a tight bomber formation was sufficient defence against fighter attacks in daylight. The Messerschmitt pilots had seemed wary of facing the Wellingtons' rear armament at a range closer than 400 yards (366 metres), and although one straggling bomber had been attacked simultaneously by four fighters it had fought its way clear without having sustained a single hit.

Designed by Dr Barnes Wallis, who was later to conceive the special mines used to breach the Möhne and Eder dams during the famus RAF raid of May 1943, the Vickers Wellington was one of the war's outstanding aircraft. In 1939, when 179 were in service with the RAF, it was certainly the best machine available to Bomber Command. Powered by two Bristol Pegasus radial engines it could carry a bomb load of 4,000 lb (1,800 kg), and later versions coould lift 6,000 lb (2,700 kg). It had a six-man crew, and defensive armament was six 0.303 in Browning machine-guns, four of them concentrated in the tail turret. In designing the Wellington, Wallis had employed geodetic construction, a method in which comparatively light strips of metal formed a web-like structure in both wings and fuselage. Apart from being light it was extremely rugged, and Wellingtons were capable of sustaining appalling battle damage and still remaining in the air.

Bomber Command was sufficiently encouraged by the result of the 3 December raid to try again. The opportunity came on the 14th, when it was reported that the cruisers *Nürnberg* and *Leipzig* had been torpedoed by a British submarine and were limping back to the Jade Estuary, badly damaged. At 11.45, twelve Wellingtons of No. 99 Squadron, led by Wing Commander J.F. Griffiths, took off from Newmarket to attack the warships. The weather was bad, with ten-tenths cloud at less than 1,000 ft (300 metres), and by the time

Vickers Wellington bombers of No 9 Squadron, RAF Bomber Command. The squadron's badge was a bat, seen here under the cockpit, and its motto Per Noctem Volamus *('We Fly by Night').* (Author's collection)

the Dutch coast was sighted at 13.05 the Wellingtons were forced to fly at 600 ft (180 metres) or less in order to stay below the overcast. The pilots had been ordered not to attack unless they could bomb from at least 2,000 ft (600 metres); they nevertheless continued on course in the hope that the cloud would lift.

By this time they were coming under heavy and continuous fire from warships and armed merchantmen lying in the approaches to the estuary. At this low altitude the bombers presented excellent targets and several were hit. Suddenly, there was a lull in the flak as enemy fighters came speeding up; they were the Messerschmitt 109s of II/JG 77, led by Major Harry von Bülow, and this time the pilots had no hesitation in pressing home their attacks up to point-blank range. The Wellingtons' gunners accounted for one Bf 109, which was seen to go down in flames, but the fighters destroyed five bombers in a matter of minutes. A sixth Wellington crashed on landing at Newmarket.

Despite the unfortunate outcome of this raid, another attack on the German fleet was planned for 18 December. Twenty-four Wellingtons of Nos 9, 37 and 149 Squadrons under the leadership of Wing Commander Kellett assembled over King's Lynn shortly after 09.00. The aircraft were loaded with 500 lb (225 kg) semi-armour-piercing bombs and the crews' orders were to attack any shipping located in the Schillig Roads, Wilhelmshaven or the Jade Estuary. The bombing level was to be at least 10,000 ft (3,000 metres).

The bombers climbed to 14,000 ft (4,250 metres) in four flights of six aircraft. Less than an hour after leaving the English coast they were flying in a cloudless sky, with visibility more than 30 miles (48 km). About two-thirds of the way across, two aircraft dropped out with engine trouble and returned to base. At 10.50 the bombers were detected by two experimental radar stations on Heligoland and Wangerooge, both equipped with the new 'Freya' detection apparatus. The officer in charge of the station on Wangerooge immediately alerted the fighter operations room at Jever, only to be told that something must be wrong with his set; the British would never be foolhardy enough to mount an attack in a cloudless sky and brilliant sunshine, where their aircraft would be sitting targets for the German fighters.

Meanwhile, the twenty-two Wellingtons had made a detour round Heligoland to avoid the anti-aircraft batteries there and were now turning in towards Wilhelmshaven from the south. After a delay of several minutes the first German fighters, six Messerschmitt 109s of 10/JG 26, led by *Oberleutnant* Johannes

Oberleutnant *Johannes Steinhoff survived a serious crash in a Messerschmitt Me 262 jet fighter in the closing weeks of the war to become Inspector-General of the postwar Luftwaffe.* (Author's collection)

Steinhoff, took off from Jever to intercept. None of the other fighter units at Jever or the adjacent airfield of Wangerooge was on readiness, and there was a further delay before these were able to take off.

Steinhoff's 109s met the Wellingtons on the approach to Wilhelmshaven and scored their first two kills almost immediately. The fighters then sheered off as the bombers flew at 13,000 ft (4,000 metres) through heavy flak over the naval base. The Wellingtons crossed Wilhelmshaven without dropping any bombs, then turned and crossed it again, still without bombing, before heading away towards the north-west. By this time, the Bf 109s of 10/JG 26 had been joined by the twin-engined Messerschmitt 110s of ZG 76 and the Bf 109s of JG 77, and the combined force of fighters now fell on the Wellington formation as it passed to the north of Wangerooge.

Another bomber went down, the victim of a Bf 110, and crash-landed on the island of Borkum. Only one member of the crew survived. Other Bf 110s accounted for five more Wellingtons in an area some fifteen miles (25 km) north-west of Borkum, and a sixth bomber was destroyed thirty miles (50 km) north of the Dutch island of Ameland. Rather belatedly, a pair of Bf 109s from JG 101 at Neumünster arrived and joined the air battle in time to catch the tail end of the Wellington formation; they shot down one bomber, but one of the Messerschmitts was badly hit and the pilot had to make a forced landing.

In one home-bound Wellington, the pilot, Sergeant J. Ramshaw, found himself sitting in an icy gale as a Bf 110's cannon shells blasted away the nose of the aircraft. The bomber was in a pitiful state; the fabric of the wings was torn and flapping in the slipstream, the metal of the engine nacelles was shredded by jagged splinters.

The rear-gunner, Leading Aircraftman Lilley, was killed outright and the front gunner, Aircraftman Driver, had his turret wrecked and the barrels of his guns shot clean away. With petrol streaming from holed fuel tanks, Sergeant Ramshaw was forced to ditch his bomber in the sea. Luckily, the survivors were picked up by a British trawler and they were put ashore safely at Grimsby the following morning. Two more Wellingtons also ditched in similar circumstances.

The raid, from which twelve bombers had failed to return, caused severe repercussions throughout RAF Bomber Command. One shortcoming in particular had contributed to the disaster; the fuel tank in the Wellington's port wing was neither self-sealing nor protected by armour plate, and when hit in this area the bombers had caught fire very rapidly. Those which did not burn lost vast quantities of fuel through holes punched in these vulnerable tanks. Within days of the raid, a priority programme was initiated to fit extra armour plate to the fuel tanks of all Bomber Command aircraft.

Most important of all, the appalling losses suffered by the Wellingtons highlighted the folly of sending bombers deep into enemy territory in broad daylight without fighter escort. After December 1939, RAF Bomber Command's policy was to operate increasingly under cover of darkness, while later in the war the Americans were to adhere to the theory that bomber formations with heavy defensive armament were capable of making successful daylight penetration attacks. The Americans, too, were destined to learn the hard way.

CHAPTER TWO

Flames Over France

When France went to war in September, 1939, the *Armée de l'Air* possessed a total of thirty-three bomber groups, of which twenty-three were stationed in metropolitan France and the rest in the colonies. The figure was still the same when, on 10 May 1940, the Germans launched their *blitzkrieg* in the west. Of the 400 bomber aircraft on the inventory of the *Armée de l'Air* at that date, 235 were in fact serviceable, but only 184 were immediately available for combat operations. Four *groupes de bombardement* were still equipped with the lumbering, twin-engined Amiot 143; first flown in April 1935, this was a re-engined version of the Amiot 140, the first of 135 examples being delivered to the

The LeO 451 was one of the finest medium bombers in the world in May 1940, but not enough were in operational service to have a telling effect against the invading German forces. (Author's collection)

Armée de l'Air in the middle of that year. The most modern bomber type in French service was the Lioré et Olivier LeO 451, also a twin-engined type; the first flight of the prototype LeO 45–01 on 16 January 1937 was followed by an initial order for twenty production LeO 451 medium bombers, and in the following two years total orders reached 749. By 10 May 1940 110 LeO 451s were on *Armée de l'Air* charge, 59 of them operational.

The latest type to enter service was an assault aircraft, the Breguet Br 693, which stemmed from a 1934 specification for a three-seat heavy fighter. In June 1938 Breguet received an order for 100 production Br 691s, but only 78 were delivered. One of these became the prototype Br 693, which first flew on 25 October 1939. French air force units were just beginning to equip with the type on 10 May 1940, when the Germans invaded. The type was powered by a pair of American Pratt & Whitney Twin Wasp radial engines.

Because of the indecision of the French high command, it was not until 11 May that the French day bombers flew their first combat sortie. This was carried out by ten LeO 451s of GB I/12 and II/12, which attacked enemy armour and transport in the Maastricht area, where vital strategic bridges over the river Maas (Meuse) had been captured intact. Nine of the bombers returned to base, although all were damaged by the intense flak and several crew members were wounded. The next daylight mission in this sector was flown by eighteen Breguet 693s of GBA I/54 and II/54, which – escorted by eighteen Morane 406 fighters of *Groupe de Chasse* III/3 – made a gallant attack on enemy columns on the Hasselt-St Trond-Liège-Maastricht area. The Breguets' combat debut had been held up because, even at this late stage, some of the aircraft still lacked bomb-release equipment; this was brought up by truck during the night of 11/12 May and hastily installed.

The attack was graphically described by Sergeant-Gunner Conill, a crew member in the leading flight of six Breguets of GBA I/54.

In front of us the Major flew his Breguet with incredible daring, skimming the roof-tops, brushing the trees, jumping obstacles. A grand game! The roofs of Tongres rose up in front of us … There was a main road, the one we were looking for, flanked by trees and ditches. And what a sight! Hundreds and hundreds of vehicles rolling towards France, following each other at short intervals and travelling fast. A lovely target! At 350 km an hour [220 mph], right down the axis of the road, flying at treetop level, the Major attacked … Suddenly white and blue flashes burst out beneath us and there was a hellish outburst of fire and steel and flames, growing more intense. I clearly saw the strings of small-calibre shells, climbing towards us by the thousand. Each of us felt that they were aimed at him personally.

Flak tore into the leading Breguet; it flicked over on a wingtip, smashed through a row of poplars and exploded in the middle of the road on top of a group of vehicles. Sergeant Conill's pilot, Lieutenant Blondy, dropped his six 100 lb (45 kg) bombs on a cluster of motorized infantry and managed to get clear with one engine on fire, racing low over the Albert Canal. Blondy belly-landed in a French field; he and his crew were among the lucky ones. In all, eight Breguets failed to return from this mission.

Then it was the turn of the RAF, ten of whose light-bomber squadrons in France, forming the Advanced Air Striking Force (AASF), were equipped with the single-engined Fairey Battle, an aircraft that was both underpowered and under-armed. Two more squadrons, Nos 114 and 139, were armed with the Bristol Blenheim medium bomber.

A foretaste of what the AASF's Fairey Battle squadrons might expect when they made contact with the *Luftwaffe* had already come on 20 September 1939, when four aircraft of No. 88 Squadron were

The Breguet 693 was a fine assault aircraft, but comparatively few were in service at the time of the German invasion and many were lost in attacks on enemy armoured columns. (Author's collection)

sent out to patrol the border. They were attacked by Messerschmitt Bf 109s over Aachen and two Battles were destroyed, although in retaliation the destruction of a 109 was claimed by Sergeant F. Letchford, the rear gunner of Battle K9243, to whom went the honour of claiming the first enemy aircraft to be destoyed by the RAF over France in the Second World War.

Ten days later, on 30 September, five Battles of No. 150 Squadron were despatched to make a reconnaissance of the Saarbrücken area. They had just penetrated enemy territory when they were attacked by eight Bf 109s. Four of the Battles were destroyed in a matter of minutes. After that, the AASF's Battles were withdrawn from daylight operations until further notice, and spent the winter months in a boring round of training and army co-operation exercises, carrying out dummy attacks on British Expeditionary Force (BEF) units in the Arras area, night cross-country flights around northern France, and practice bombing sorties.

On 10 May 1940, when the German offensive opened on the Western Front, most of the AASF's squadrons had been at readiness since 06.00, with half their available aircraft ready for take-off at thirty minutes' notice and half at two hours' notice. However, the German advance was so rapid that Allied intelligence was unable to keep pace with the enemy's movements, and it was not until midday that firm target information was available. A few minutes later, thirty-two Battles – one flight each from Nos 12, 103, 105, 142, 150, 218 and 226

Fairey Battle light bombers of No. 88 Squadron, RAF Advanced Air Striking Force, in formation with Curtiss Hawk fighters of Groupe de Chasse GC I/5. The Battles suffered horrendous casualties in the Battle of France. (ECP Armées)

Squadrons – took off from their respective bases with orders to attack enemy columns advancing through Luxembourg. They approached the target in four waves of eight aircraft, escorted by five Hawker Hurricanes of No. 1 Squadron and three of No. 73 Squadron, which broke away and patrolled over the city of Luxembourg itself. The Battles made their attack and encountered no enemy fighters, but they ran into a blizzard of fire from quadruple 20 mm anti-aircraft guns – the formidable *Flakvierling* – and heavy machine guns, and thirteen of them were shot down. All the others were damaged to some extent.

At 15.30 the AASF mounted a second attack on the columns of the German Sixteenth Army in Luxembourg, again with thirty-two Battles. This time there was no fighter escort, and a squadron of Bf 109s came tumbling down on the British bombers. Ten Battles failed to return from this sortie. Twenty-three aircraft out of sixty-four, with as many again damaged so badly as to be out of action for some time, was a fearful rate of attrition, and the AASF flew no more combat sorties that day. On the 11th one low-level attack by eight Battles, drawn from Nos 88 and 218 Squadrons, was ordered against enemy forces moving up to the Luxembourg border, but it is doubtful whether they even reached the target area. The only crew to return, their aircraft badly hit by anti-aircraft fire, reported seeing three other Battles go down in heavy flak while still over the Ardennes.

At 11.30 on 11 May, nine Fairey Battles of the Belgian air force's 5/III/3 *Escadrille*, operating from Aeltre, took off to attack the three bridges over the Albert Canal at Veldwezelt, Vroenhoven and Briedgen, in the area of Maastricht, over which the armour of 16th Panzerkorps was pouring. The mission was a disaster; six of the Battles were shot down before they got anywhere near their targets, and the 100 lb (45 kg) bombs of the surviving three failed to do any damage.

By mid-morning on 12 May the AASF's two Bristol Blenheim medium bomber squadrons had been practically annihilated, which meant that the vulnerable Battle units would once again have to be sent into action in daylight. Air Marshal Barratt, commanding the British Air Forces in France, was well aware that such a course of action would mean virtual suicide for the Battle crews, but he had no choice but to commit them. However, he stressed that an attack on the bridges was to be strictly a job for volunteers.

One hundred and twenty miles (190 km) from Maastricht, not far from Reims, lay the little grass airfield of Amifontaine, the base of No. 12 Squadron. Shortly after 08.00 on this beautiful Sunday morning, the squadron's crews – thirty young men in total – were

crammed into the small operations hut listening in silence as the
deputy commanding officer, Squadron Leader Lowe, told them that
the squadron had been selected to send six volunteer crews against
the bridges at Vroenhoven and Veldwezelt. With the whole
squadron clamouring to be given the chance to go, Lowe finally
settled for the six crews already on standby. Three Battles would
attack the bridge at Veldwezelt, and three the bridge at Vroenhoven.
The former was to be the objective of 'B' Flight, led by twenty-two-
year-old Flying Officer Donald ('Judy') Garland, whose opposite
number in 'A' Flight was Flying Officer Norman Thomas, who
would lead the attack on the Vroenhoven bridge.

Thomas was the first to take off, followed by Pilot Officer Davy.
The third member of 'A' Flight, Pilot Officer Brereton, had
mechanical trouble with his aircraft and had to be left behind (in
fact, he tried three aircraft and found them all unserviceable). Five
minutes later, Garland's Battle was also airborne, followed by the
two machines piloted by Flying Officer McIntosh and Sergeant Fred
Marland. Thomas and Davy climbed steadily at 160 mph (250 kph),
levelling off at 7,000 ft (2,100 metres). Scattered cloud was creeping
across the sky from the east. Thomas glanced at his watch: it was
09.00, and Tongeren was dead ahead. At that moment a heavy flak
barrage erupted around the Battles. It came as a nasty surprise;
there had been no indication that the Germans had advanced this
far. Thomas and Davy came down to 5,000 ft (1,500 metres) and
altered course north-east, heading straight for the target.

Five minutes ahead of the Battles, the eight Hurricanes of No. 1
Squadron were also heading for Maastricht. Two more Hurricane
squadrons, Nos 85 and 87 of the BEF Air Component, had also been
detailed to provide fighter escort, but No. 1 was the first on the scene.
High over the Albert Canal, the fighter pilots caught sight of a swarm
of glittering crosses. They were the Messerschmitt 109s of 3
Jagdgeschwader – almost 100 fighters. Without hesitating, No. 1
Squadron's commanding officer, Squadron Leader Halahan, gave the
order to attack. After a brief, one-sided dogfight, the wreckage of six
Hurricanes and three 109s lay burning on the banks of the canal.

Under cover of the diversion, Thomas roared over the
Maastricht–Tongeren road towards his objective, the concrete
bridge at Vroenhoven. A Bf 109 appeared away to starboard and
began to close in, but Thomas held his course. Then the enemy
fighter turned and went after Davy, who sheered off into a cloud.
The flak was coming up thick and fast now. Thomson pointed the
Battle's nose at the bridge ahead and eased forward the control

columnn. The altimeter unwound rapidly and at 3,000 ft (900 metres) Thomas pressed the bomb release. One of his 250-pounders dropped away, followed by the other three, singly. The Battle came out of its dive and raced across the canal at less than 100 ft (30 metres), hit again and again by shells. Thomas skipped over a German convoy, then the engine died and he brought the aircraft down for a belly landing. Dazed but unhurt, the crew scrambled out of the wreck and were taken prisoner.

Diving behind his leader, having managed to shake off the 109, Pilot Officer Davy saw Thomas's bombs erupt on the far end of the bridge. He dropped his own bombs from 2,000 ft (600 metres) and, to his disappointment, saw them explode in the water and on the canal bank. He turned away and raced for safety, chased by the flak, and at that moment he was attacked by a 109. His rear gunner damaged the fighter and drove it off, but not before cannon shells had set fire to the port fuel tank. Davy ordered his crew to bale out, and was about to follow them over the side when the fire suddenly went out. He nursed the crippled aircraft towards base, and was only a few miles from home when he ran out of fuel and had to come down in a field. A few hours later Sergeant Mansell, Davy's observer, arrived back at Amifontaine; Patterson, the gunner, had not been so lucky. He came down behind the German lines and spent the rest of the war in a prisoner of war (PoW) camp.

The bridge at Vroenhoven still stood. Five minutes after Thomas's attack, Garland's flight was approaching its metal twin at Veldwezelt. Garland favoured a low-level attack, and the three Battles swept across the Belgian landscape at 50 ft (15 metres). In line astern they plunged into the writhing cloud of flak bursts. Flying Officer McIntosh's aircraft was hit almost immediately and burst into flames; despite severe burns, the pilot managed to jettison his bombs and made a perfect belly landing on the left bank of the canal. The crew, all injured, got clear and were taken prisoner.

A Battle staggered out of the smoke, burning from wingtip to wingtip. It was Fred Marland's aircraft. It went into a steep climb, then flicked over and dived vertically into the ground. There were no survivors. The third Battle – Garland's – suddenly appeared over the bridge, turning steeply, shedding fragments as the flak hit it. Leaving a thin trail of smoke, it dived at the western end of the bridge, dropped its bombs successfully, then crashed to earth beside the canal.

Although Garland's action had severely damaged the Veldwezelt bridge, German sappers quickly bypassed the damage by building a pontoon bridge alongside and the flow of traffic was soon on the move again. Perhaps the entire operation, gallant though it was, was best summed up in the words of a German officer who interrogated Flying Officer McIntosh's shot-down crew: 'You British are mad. We capture the bridge early Friday morning. You give us all Friday and Saturday to get our flak guns up in circles all around the bridge, and then on Sunday, when all is ready, you come along with three aircraft and try to blow the thing up.'

Garland and his observer, Segeant Tom Gray, were posthumously awarded the RAF's first two Victoria Crosses of the Second World War. Their gunner, Leading Aircraftman Roy Reynolds, received a posthumous promotion to the rank of corporal. That he received no medal was excused by the fact that, unlike the other two crew members, he had 'not been occupying a decision-making position'. It was an omission that left a bitter taste in the mouths of his relatives and squadron comrades for a long time afterwards.

Later in the day, twenty-four Blenheims of No. 2 Group, RAF Bomber Command, tried to attack the Meuse bridges that lay within the perimeter of Maastricht. Ten of them failed to return. Six more Battles were also lost during the afternoon in the course of fifteen sorties against enemy concentrations in the Bouillon sector. During the day's operations, 62 per cent of the Battles despatched on combat sorties had fallen victim to enemy flak and fighters.

By the morning of 13 May it was becoming clear that the main German thrust was aimed at the Sedan sector, at the northern end of the Maginot Line, and Air Marshal Barratt was already deluged with appeals for help from the French general headquarters. Barratt, however, was determined that his bomber squadrons – whose effective strength had been reduced from 135 to 72 aircraft in the space of forty-eight hours- should not be sent into action again unless really worthwhile targets had been found for them. Accordingly, only one small bombing mission was carried out by the AASF on 13 May, when a small number of Battles of No. 226 Squadron bombed a factory in an attempt to block the road at Breda at the request of the French Seventh Army, which was pulling back towards Antwerp under heavy pressure from the 9th *Panzer* Division.

By nightfall on the 13th the German 1st Rifle Regiment and elements of the 2nd *Panzer* Division had forced crossings of the Meuse over pontoon bridges near Sedan, assisted by strong air support. In the early hours of the 14th General Billotte, commanding the French First Group of Armies, telephoned Air

Marshal Barratt and begged him to send the AASF into action in the Sedan area. 'Victory or defeat hinges on the destruction of those bridges,' the French general emphasized. Barratt accordingly authorized the AASF to attack the pontoons across the Meuse, and the first two missions of this kind – carried out at 04.30 and 06.30 by two flights of five Battles drawn from Nos 103 and 150 Squadrons – were encouraging; all the bombers returned safely to base.

A few of the pontoons appeared to have been damaged, but the *panzers* continued to rumble across into the bridgehead established on the west bank the previous evening. Further north, the 6th *Panzer* Division pushed through a second breach in the Monthermé area, while in the Dinant sector General Erwin Rommel's 7th *Panzer* Division poured into a third bridgehead. During the morning and early afternoon the French threw all their available bombers against these objectives. The first French mission of the day was flown at 09.00 by eight surviving Breguet 693s of *GBA 18*, which made a low-level attack on pontoons between Douzy and Vrigne-sur-Meuse and on enemy armoured columns in the Bazeilles area. The Breguets, which were escorted by fifteen RAF Hurricanes and fifteen Bloch 152 fighters of GC I/8, encountered only light flak and their strong fighter escort kept the Messerschmitts at arm's length.

Meanwhile, eighteen elderly Amiot 143 night bombers of *Groupements* 9 and 10 had also been ordered to stand by for a mission in the Sedan sector. The crews were originally briefed for a mission against the Meuse bridges, but at the last moment the orders were changed; the target was now to be the enemy columns that congested the roads. After three nights of maximum-effort operations the Amiot groups were in a pitiful condition; most of their aircraft were worn out and there were very few spares.

The eighteen Amiots took off at 11.25 from their respective bases at la Ferté-Gaucher and Nangis, flown by volunteer crews. Each machine carried sixteen 100 lb (45 kg) and two 220 lb (100 kg) bombs. Their fighter escort was to be provided by twelve Morane 406s of GC III/7, twelve Bloch 152s of GC I/8 and nine Dewoitine 520s of GC I/3. In the event, six Amiots failed to make rendezvous with the fighters and turned back on the order of their commander.

The remainder pressed on towards their targets in the Sedan-Givonne-Bazeille sector. Over la Fère airfield they picked up their close escort of twelve Moranes; the other fighters were sweeping the sky a few minutes ahead, at high altitude. At 12.15 the formation passed to the south of Mezières, flying at 1,000 ft (300 metres) under

*The Amiot 143 heavy bomber was obsolete in May 1940, but such was
the desperate nature of the situation that it was thrown into action
against the Meuse bridges in broad daylight.* (ECP Armées)

a cover of six-tenths cloud. A few minutes later the bombers and their
escort were over the broad ribbon of the Meuse, and a gentle turn to
starboard brought them in towards Sedan from the north. So far, it
was like a peacetime training flight; the sky was absolutely empty.

Suddenly, the sky was filled with flak bursts and glowing trails
of 20 mm shells. An Amiot was hit and began to drag a long ribbon
of flame. It was an aircraft of GB II/34, piloted by Lieutenant
Vauzelle, and it carried II/34's commander, Commandant de
Laubier. At the last moment, as the machine had been taxiing out
for take-off, de Laubier had jumped aboard and had taken the place
of one of the gunners. Now, thirty minutes later, the other crews
watched in horror as the Amiot plunged earthwards like a torch.
Three of the crew baled out and were taken prisoner; de Laubier
and Vauzelle were not among them.

At that moment, six Amiots of GB II/38 broke formation abruptly
and turned in the direction of the Meuse bridges, their crews
apparently unaware that the target had been changed. This

manoeuvre presented the fighter escort, which now had two separate formations to cover, with an unexpected problem. The Moranes split into two flights of six, one of which chased after II/38. The other six Amiots continued their run-in and unloaded their bombs on the congested roads north of Sedan, lurching as flak hit them again and again. One machine broke formation, trailing smoke, and began a descending turn towards friendly territory. Despite being attacked by an enemy fighter the pilot, Lieutenant Foucher, managed to regain his base after flying the whole way at treetop height.

As the bombers roared out of the flak zone, throttles wide open, the Messerschmitts pounced. A pair of Bf 110s fastened themselves on to the tails of the two surviving Amiots of II/34, one of which was quickly shot down in flames. The five-man crew baled out. The other aircraft received three 20 mm shells in its port engine, which began to stream dense white smoke; a fourth shell shattered the port undercarriage, a fifth ripped the pilot's parachute pack to shreds and a sixth tore away the co-pilot's control column. The pilot, *Adjudant* Milan, made his escape into a bank of cumulus and crash-landed in a field a few minutes later. The crew all got out safely, but the aircraft was a complete write-off.

By some miracle, all the other Amiots in the Sedan operation returned to base, although all of them were shot to ribbons and not one was in a battleworthy condition. A simultaneous attack had been made in the same area by eight unescorted LeO 451s of *Groupement* 6; one received a direct flak hit in the bomb bay and exploded in mid-air. The other seven got away, but in their case too battle damage rendered them all unserviceable.

When the attacks were over the French bomber force was exhausted; there were no more reserves. Up to this point the AASF commander, Air Vice-Marshal Playfair, following Air Marshal Barratt's instructions, had been holding his squadrons in reserve to give them a few more hours in which to scrape together their available resources; these amounted to only sixty-two Battles and eight Blenheims, but with the French bomber force ineffective Barratt and Playfair had no alternative but to commit these battered remnants.

Between 15.00 and 16.00 that afternoon, the AASF threw every aircraft that could still fly into the cauldron. It was a massacre. No. 12 Squadron lost four aircraft out of five; No. 142 four out of eight; No. 226 three out of six; No. 105 six out of eleven; No. 150 lost all four; No. 88 one out of ten; No. 103 three out of eight and

No. 218 ten out of eleven. Of the eight Blenheims sent out by 114 and 139 Squadrons, only three returned to base. It was the highest loss in an operation of similar size ever experienced by the RAF, and all that was achieved was the destruction of two pontoon bridges and the damaging of two more. During the days that followed, six Battle crews, all shot down behind enemy lines, managed to struggle back to their bases. They included a pilot who, although wounded in two places, had managed to swim the Meuse; and an observer and gunner who had remained with their badly injured pilot in enemy territory for more than twenty-four hours, leaving him only when he died. All the other crews – 102 young men – were either dead or prisoners.

At dusk, the pontoons were again attacked by twenty-eight Blenheims of No. 2 Group. Seven aircraft failed to return, including two which crash-landed in French territory.

With the AASF shattered, the brunt of the RAF's bombing offensive against the Meuse bridgeheads on 15 May had to be borne by the home-based squadrons of Bomber Command. In the

Bristol Blenheim Mk IV of No. 139 Squadron over France. Together with No. 114 Squadron, No. 139 formed the medium bomber component of the Advanced Air Striking Force. (IWM)

morning the German forces broke through at Sedan, and at 11.00 twelve Blenheims of No. 2 Group attacked enemy columns in the Dinant area while 150 French fighters flew patrols in relays over the battlefield. Sixteen more Blenheims, escorted by twenty-seven French fighters, made an attack at 15.00 on bridges in the Samoy region and on enemy armour at Monthermé and Mezières; four Blenheims failed to return. What was left of the Battles made only one operational sortie, a small-scale raid on enemy positions in the Sedan bridgehead after dark.

By 19 May, with the Germans breaking through the Allied defences everywhere and the *Luftwaffe* in control of the sky, daylight operations by both the AASF and No. 2 Group over France had come to a virtual standstill, although the Battles and Blenheims continued to fly night bombing missions. There was a brief resumption of day bombing by the Battles after 3 June, when they

Fast low-level attacks on enemy columns were also made by Latecoere 298 dive-bombers of the French Naval Air Arm. These aircraft, too, suffered crippling losses. (ECP Armées)

made several attacks from new locations near Le Mans on railways at Givet and Charleville, fuel and ammunition dumps at Florenville and Libramont, troop concentrations at St Gobain and Gault and advanced German airstrips at St Hubert and Guise. The last major daylight attack by the AASF was carried out on 13 June, when forty-eight Battles struck at troop concentrations along the Seine and Marne. Six aircraft failed to return. Two days later, with armistice negotiations in progress between the French and German governments, the squadrons were ordered to evacuate their remaining aircraft to England. The French fought on for a few more days, but their position was hopeless. The Battle of France was over.

CHAPTER THREE

Fighter-bombers against England

On 7 July 1940, a special *Luftwaffe* unit was formed at Köln-Ostheim under the command of *Hauptmann* Walter Rubensdörffer. Equipped with a mixture of single-engined Messerschmitt Bf 109s and twin-engined Bf 110s, its task was to pioneer the tactics that would be employed by the Bf 110's successor, the Messerschmitt Me 210 – hence the new unit's designation of *Erprobungsgruppe* ('Trials Group') 210, or EGr 210.

The Messerschmitt Me 210, seen here, had a protracted development history and was not a success. Erprobungsgruppe 210 *was formed to pioneer its entry into service.* (Bundesarchiv)

One of the unit's *Staffeln*, I/EGr. 210 was equipped with the Messerschmitt Bf 110C, and was activated by simply renumbering I/*Zerstörergeschwader* 1; similarly, III/*Stukageschwader* 77, which was armed with the Messerschmitt Bf 110D, became II/EGr. 210. The group's third *Staffel*, which had Messerschmitt Bf 109Es, was previously IV/*Trägergruppe* 186, which had been designated as the fighter element of the air group intended for the aircraft carrier *Graf Zeppelin*, on which work had been halted.

Walter Rubensdörffer was of Swiss origin, having been born at Basle in 1910. He had joined the new *Luftwaffe* in the early 1930s and had subsequently fought with the German Condor Legion in the Spanish Civil War, flying Heinkel He 51 biplanes on ground attack work.

Rubensdörffer was destined never to fly the Me 210, which was plagued by development problems from its inception in 1937, when the German air ministry (*Reichsluftministerium*, or RLM) approved the project and took the unusual step of ordering 1,000 examples off the drawing board. The prototype, initially fitted with twin fins and rudders, flew for the first time on 2 September 1939 and showed serious stability problems. The twin fins were replaced by a single fin assembly, which improved matters somewhat, but not much.

Although the service debut of the Me 210 would now be seriously delayed, the *Oberkommando der Luftwaffe* (OKL) decided to proceed with the use of the Bf 109 and Bf 110 in the fighter-bomber role. Following the installation of bomb shackles, permitting the aircraft to carry either SC250 or SC500 bombs, EGr 210 moved to its main operating base of Denain in France, from where it deployed aircraft to its forward base at Calais-Marck on the Channel coast for operations against the British Isles.

These began almost at once, the Messerschmitts carrying out dive-bombing attacks on British shipping in the Channel, and the unit's first casualty was sustained on Saturday, 13 July 1940, when a Bf 110 was seriously damaged in combat with RAF fighters and had to crash-land at St Omer. Its crew suffered no injury, despite the fact that their aircraft was 45 per cent wrecked. On the 18th, another of the group's Bf 110s dived vertically into the ground near Antwerp, one of its crew being killed. On the 24th, yet another Bf 110, engaged in a shipping attack, exploded in mid-air off Harwich, the probable victim of anti-aircraft fire. This time, both crew were killed. Two days later EGr. 210 lost a fourth Bf 110, which dived into the sea at high speed after being hit by anti-aircraft (A A) fire at 2,000 ft (610 metres); its pilot, *Oberleutnant* Fallenbacher, and his observer were killed.

The *Gruppe* was now suffering losses on an almost daily basis. On 29 July, Bf 110C-6 S9+TH of I/EGr. 210 was attacked by a Hawker Hurricane of No. 151 Squadron (Flying Officer Blair) as it attempted to bomb a convoy off Orfordness and badly damaged, its pilot, *Leutnant* Beudel, made an emergency landing at St Omer with a wounded gunner.

On the 30th, *I Staffel* lost another Bf 110, shot down 19 miles (30 km) east of Harwich by Flight Lieutenant Hamilton and Sergeant Allard of No. 85 Squadron, also flying Hurricanes. *Leutnant* Herold and his observer were killed.

During the first week of August 1940 the *Gruppe* was withdrawn from anti-shipping operations to concentrate on honing its dive-bombing skills. Despite its absence from the combat area, losses continued; on 6 August a Bf 110 of II/EGr. 210 dived into the sea off Denain during dive-bombing practice, and a second crashed on a routine test flight. In each case, both crew members were killed. The next day, the *Gruppe* lost its first Bf 109, when an aircraft flown by *Hauptmann* Valesi crashed off Denain, killing its pilot.

Back in action again on 11 August, attacking shipping off Harwich, I/EGr. 210 lost two Bf 110s in combat with RAF fighters. The two pilots, *Gefreiter* Weiss and *Leutnant* Bertram, were both killed, along with their observers.

Principal equipment of Erprobungsgruppe 210 *was the Messerschmitt Bf 110. It suffered badly at the hands of the RAF's Spitfires and Hurricanes.* (Author's collection)

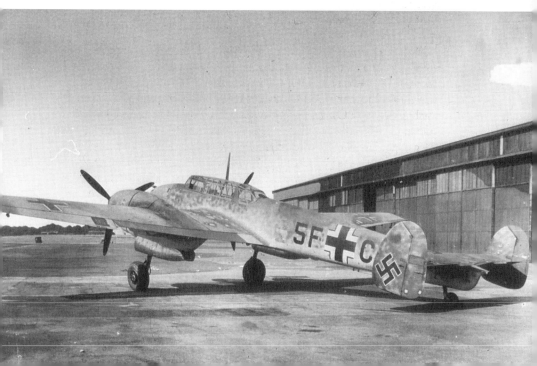

Erprobungsgruppe 210 was now about to face its biggest test so far, for it had a key role to play in the German air onslaught that was about to be hurled against Britain. The organization which RAF Fighter Command now had in place to meet that onslaught was far different from that with which the RAF had very nearly gone to war two years earlier, at the time of the Munich crisis of 1938. Under the determined and energetic leadership of 54-year-old Air Chief Marshal Sir Hugh Dowding, Fighter Command had become a tightly knit defensive network, where control and standardization were the keywords.

Dowding's approach was essentially a scientific one; he believed that Britain's air defences should have the benefit of the latest technological developments. This was reflected in Fighter Command's operations rooms, linked with one another by an elaborate system of telephone and teleprinter lines to provide an integrated system of control. This enabled fighter aircraft to be passed rapidly from sector to sector and from group to group, wherever they were most needed.

Nowhere was modern technology more apparent in Britain's defences than in the use of radar – or radio direction-finding (RDF) as it was then known. Developed by Robert Watson-Watt from earlier experiments in thunderstorm detection by the use of radio waves, the use of radar as an integral part of the British air defence system was largely the fruit of Dowding's initiative; he had worked with Watson-Watt during the 1930s and had not been slow to recognize the potential of the new invention. The Germans had made several determined efforts to ferret out Britain's radar secrets before the war with the aid of special radio equipment installed in commercial airliners and the airship *Graf Zeppelin*, but reconnaissance of this kind had come to a virtual standstill after the outbreak of war, and the erection of the chain of radar masts along the southern and eastern coasts of Britain had continued unmolested.

The Germans recognized that the destruction of the radar stations was a vital preliminary to the main air offensive against southern England. Planning for the offensive was completed by 2 August 1940; *Luftflotten* ('Air Fleets') 2 and 3 were to attack simultaneously, their main task being to bring the British fighters to combat, to destroy the coastal fighter airfields and the radar stations, and to disrupt the RAF's ground organization in southern England. On the second day the attacks would be extended to airfields around London, and would continue at maximum effort throughout the third day. The *Luftwaffe* High Command hoped in this way to

The primary targets for Erprogunsgruppe *210 at the onset of the Battle of Britain were the all-important radar stations on England's south coast.* (Author's collection)

weaken the RAF by a few decisive blows, so establishing the air superiority necessary for any further operations.

To carry out this task the *Luftwaffe* had three *Luftflotten*. *Luftflotte* 2, under General Kesselring, was based in Holland, Belgium and north-eastern France, *Luftflotte* 3, under general Sperrle, in northern and north-western France; and *Luftflotte* 5, under General Stumpff, in Norway and Denmark. Together their resources amounted to some 3,500 aircraft, of which 2,250 – 1,000 medium bombers, 1,000 fighters and 250 dive-bombers – were serviceable. To counter this force, Air Chief Marshal Dowding had 704 serviceable fighters, including 620 Hurricanes and Spitfires.

Everything was fixed except the date. To carry out its allotted tasks the *Luftwaffe* needed at least three days of continuous good weather. A fine spell was expected to continue during the first week of August, but the *Luftflotten* were unable to take advantage of it as they needed another week to make final preparations for the great onslaught. At last the *Lufwaffe* was ready and *Adlertag* – Eagle Day – was fixed for 10 August, but then the weather took a sudden turn for the worse and it had to be postponed. On 11 August the weather forecast for the next few days looked more promising; the final decision was made and *Adlertag* was scheduled for 13 August.

On the morning of 12 August, twenty-four hours before the main offensive was due to begin, twenty-one Messerschmitt 109s and 110s of *Erprobungsgruppe* 210 took off from Calais-Marck airfield and set course at low level over the English Channel. As they approached the English coast they climbed and split up, heading for their individual targets. *I Staffel*, comprising six Bf 110s led by *Oberleutnant* Martin Lutz, attacked the radar station at Pevensey, near Eastbourne, each aircraft dropping two 1,000 lb (450 kg) bombs, causing damage to installations and power cables but leaving the four masts intact. Under *Oberleutnant* Rössiger, *II Staffel* dive-bombed the radar station at Rye, near Hastings, also causing substantial damage to installations, while the Bf 109s of *Oberleutnant* Otto Hintze's *III Staffel* swept down on Dover, with similar results. Despite the damage, however, all three stations were operational again within three hours.

It was a different story at Ventnor, on the Isle of Wight, where the radar station was attacked thirty minutes later by fifteen Junkers Ju 88s. Their bombing was extremely accurate and the station was damaged beyond repair. To cover up the dangerous gap created by the loss of the Ventnor station, the British transmitted a false signal on the wrecked station's frequency; the German listening posts on the other side of the Channel consequently believed that Ventnor was still fully operational. In fact, it was only after eleven days of non-stop work that another station was brought into action on the Isle of Wight.

In the afternoon of 12 August, EGr. 210 attacked the forward airfield of Manston with twenty Messerschmitts. Manston was temporarily disabled. All the Messerschmitts returned to Calais-Marck unscathed with the exception of one, which crash-landed near Calais and was written off after an engagement with RAF fighters over the Channel.

Erprobungsgruppe 210 did not participate in operations on *Adlertag* itself, but it was back in action on Wednesday, 14 August, a day in which air operations were hampered by bad weather. Once again, Manston was the target. The attack was carried out by the Bf 110Ds of I *Staffel*, and on this occasion two 110s fell victim to Manston's anti-aircraft defences, three of the four crew members being killed.

The next day, 15 August, was disastrous for EGr. 210. In the early evening, fifteen Bf 110s and eight Bf 109s set course over the Channel to attack the airfield at Kenley, south of London, but they made a navigational error and attacked Croydon by mistake, destroying forty training aircraft. As they were making their attack they were engaged by the Hurricanes of Nos 32 and 111 Squadrons. The first to go, at 18.50, was Bf 110D S9+CB, which crash-landed at School Farm, Hooe, after being attacked by a Hurricane. The crew, *Leutnant* Koch and *Unteroffizier* Kahl, survived and were taken prisoner.

Walter Rubensdörffer was an early casualty, his aircraft (Bf 110D S9+AB) crashing in flames on Bletchinglye Farm, Rotherfield. The pilot and his observer, *Obergefreiter* Kretzer, were both killed. The time was 19.00. Also at this time, a Bf 110C-6 of II *Staffel* was attacked and shot down by Squadron Leader Worrall and Flight Lieutenant Crossley of No. 32 Squadron, crashing at Ightham. The pilot, *Leutnant* Ortner, baled out wounded and was captured, but his observer, *Obergefreiter* Lohmann, was killed.

The other Messerschmitts were harried mercilessly as they fled for the coast. At 19.10, Bf 110C-6 S9+TH of I *Staffel* was shot down by Flight Lieutenant Connors and Sergeant Wallace of 111 Squadron, crashing at Broadbridge Farm, Horley, and killing its crew, *Leutnant* Beudel and *Obergefreiter* Jordan; while Bf 110D S9+CK of II *Staffel* crashed at Hawkhurst after a fighter attack. Its crew, *Oberleutnant* Habisch and *Unteroffizier* Elfner, were captured. Five minutes later, Bf 110D S9+BB of EGr. 210's Staff Flight was shot down by Sergeant Dymond of No. 111 Squadron and Sergeant Pearce of No. 32, crashing on Nutfield aerodrome. The pilot, *Oberleutnant* Fiedeler – the *Gruppe* Adjutant – was killed, but his observer, *Unteroffizier* Werner, was captured alive. Also taken prisoner was *Leutnant* Marx, *Staffelkapitän* of 3/EGr. 210, whose Bf 109 was shot down at Frant.

On the following day, command of *Erprobungsgruppe* 210 was assumed by *Hauptmann* Hans von Boltenstern, and operations continued at a reduced rate for the next few days until the *Gruppe* was brought up to strength again. On 31 August, II *Staffel* suffered two aircraft damaged, although both returned to Calais-Marck, but a third (Bf 110D S9+GK) was forced down at Wrotham Hill on the

southern outskirts of London. One crew member was killed, the
other captured.

Hans von Boltenstern's tenure as *Kommandeur* of EGr. 210 was
short-lived; on Wednesday, 4 September 1940, his Bf 110D S9+AB
was shot down into the Channel and he was killed, along with his
observer, *Feldwebel* Schneider. He was succeeded by *Hauptmann*
Martin Lutz. On 6 September, the day after Lutz took over, the
Gruppe lost another aircraft, when Bf 110D S9+BH of I *Staffel* was
shot down near Oxted, Surrey, after attacking Redhill aerodrome.
The pilot, *Unteroffizier* Rüger, was killed; his obsever, *Unteroffizier*
Ernst, was captured wounded. On the next day, a Bf 109 pilot of III
Staffel had a lucky escape when he was rescued by the *Seenotdienst*
(German air-sea rescue service) after being shot down into the
Channel.

Hit-and-run bombing attacks against targets on the English coast
continued. On Tuesday, 24 September, Bf 110D S9+HH was shot

*The Junkers Ju 87 Stuka dive-bomber was also used for precision attacks
on airfields and other targets in southern England. It was quickly
withdrawn from the battle after sustaining unacceptable casualties.*
(Author's collection)

down into the sea by AA fire off Southampton Water; the bodies of the crew, *Leutnant* von der Horst and *Obergefreiter* Ollers, were never recovered.

Friday, 27 September, was another bad day for the *Gruppe*, which launched an attack on targets in the Bristol area around midday. Four Bf 110s were lost, including that (S9+DH) of the *Gruppe Kommandeur*, Martin Lutz. Under attack by fighters, he crashed into some trees at Bussey Stool farm, Cranbourne Chase, near Shaftsbury. He and his observer, *Unteroffizier* Schön, were killed. Also killed were *Leutnant* Schmidt and *Feldwebel* Richter in Bf 110D S9+JH, which went down at Bradle Row, Kimmeridge, after a fighter attack. Luckier were *Feldwebel* Ebner and Gefreiter Zwick in S9+DU, who were captured wounded after being shot down by fighters at The Beeches, Preston Hill, Iwerne Minster; but the *Staffelkapitän*, *Oberleutnant* Rössiger, and his observer, *Oberfeldwebel* Marx, were both listed as missing after their aircraft was shot down over the sea. Only one of the original *Staffelkapitän* was left now, and *Hauptmann* Otto Hintze took over as *Gruppe Kommandeur*. The Gruppe suffered further losses on 5 October, when two more Bf 110s were destroyed and two damaged.

By this time, with the *Luftwaffe's* medium bomber force suffering unacceptable losses in daylight attacks and the main offensive switching to night operations, the fighter-bomber tactics pioneered by EGr. 210 were adopted by other fighter units, and October 1940 saw an increase in fighter-bomber operations against southern England. To counter these new methods, RAF Fighter Command initiated high-level standing patrols on a line covering Biggin Hill-Maidstone-Gravesend. On 8 October the Germans made several small-scale fighter-bomber attacks on London, and the next day, slipping across the Channel under cover of cloud and rain, the fighter-bombers made sporadic attacks on RAF airfields in the south-east. On 10 October enemy fighter-bombers came over south-east England in streams, and Fighter Command pilots reported extreme difficulty in intercepting them because of heavy showers interspersed with dazzling bright intervals.

On 12 October, Adolf Hitler issued an order postponing his planned invasion of Britain until the following spring. The pilots of Fighter Command knew nothing of this tacit admission of defeat, and on that day they were busy warding off attacks on Biggin Hill and Kenley, losing ten aircraft against the *Luftwaffe's* eleven. On the 15th the weather was fine, and a morning attack on London by Bf 109 fighter-bombers wrecked the approach to Waterloo station and temporarily closed the railway lines. Factories on the south bank of the Thames were badly hit, and in the evening a major attack by medium bombers wrecked parts of the docks and Paddington, Victoria, Waterloo and Liverpool Street stations. The *Luftwaffe*'s loss of fourteen aircraft that day included eight Bf 109s, destroyed in a 'bounce' by RAF fighters. Attacks by high-flying fighter-bombers, operating in streams or in massed raids, continued throughout the remainder of October, the 29th being a particularly active day, with heavy attacks on RAF airfields and coastal targets. The *Luftwaffe*'s combat loss of twenty aircraft included five Bf 109s of JG 51, bounced by RAF fighters as a result of good tactical planning.

From now on, because of increasingly bad weather and the fact that the *Luftwaffe* had exhausted its tactical options, the daylight offensive against Britain began to peter out. Although daylight incrusions would continue for the rest of the year, weather permitting, to all intents and purposes the Battle of Britain was over. The *Luftwaffe* had been rebuffed, its tactical advantages ruined by inept political and military decisions.

As for *Erprobungsgruppe* 210, the unit, now under the command of *Major* Wilhelm-Otto Lessmann, remained in the Channel area until 24 April 1941, ultimately based on Abbeville, when it was redesignated *Schnellkampfgeschwader* 210 (SKG 210). A month later it moved to Poland under Major Walter Storp for the start of the campaign in Russia. In April 1942 it was absorbed into *Zerstörergeschwader* I, disbanding in July 1944.

The transfer of air units to the Eastern Front , the Balkans and North Africa in the summer of 1941 left the *Luftwaffe*'s assets in the Channel area seriously depleted, the fighter resources being reduced to just two *Jagdgeschwader*, *Major* Walter Oesau's JG. 2 '*Richthofen*' and *Oberstleutnant* Adolf Galland's JG. 26 '*Schlageter*', both equipped with the Messerschmitt Bf 109E-7, F-2 and F-4. In August 1941 the first Focke-Wulf Fw 190A-1 was delivered to II/JG. 26, and gradually this excellent fighter began to supplant the Jagdgeschwader's Bf 109s, but JG.2 did not began to receive Focke-Wulfs for some time afterwards.

In November 1941 two fighter-bomber *Staffeln* were created within JG. 2 and JG. 26, designated 10(*Jabo*)/JG. 2 and 10 (*Jabo*)/ JG. 26 respectively. Both were armed with the Bf 109F-4/B, which was fitted with an under-fuselage rack for a 500 lb (225 kg) SC250 bomb. After a series of experimental low-level attacks against British coastal targets and shipping in the winter of 1941–42, both units were officially sanctioned by *General* Hugo Sperrle, commanding

Luftflotte 3, on 10 March 1942. Often taking advantage of poor visibility, JG. 26's aircraft would take off from their well-defended bases at Abbeville, Ligescourt, Poix or St Omer and streak across the Channel at wavetop height to avoid radar detection, their principal targets being port facilities and gasholders. 10 (*Jabo*)/JG. 2, based further south around Evreux and Caen, also specialized in attacks on British shipping in the Channel. Up to 26 July, 1942, 10 (*Jabo*)/JG. 26 claimed the destruction of eight railway installations, eight barracks, six ships, five factories, two gasholders and two harbour installations, while 10 (*Jabo*)/JG. 2 claimed to have sunk twenty ships totalling some 63,000 tons (64,000 tonnes). Because of the element of surprise, the losses sustained by the fighter-bomber units during this period were very light, and it was not until 24 April that 10/JG. 2 lost its first Messerschmitt, in an attack on a gas holder at Folkestone.

By September 1942 the two fighter-bomber units had rearmed with the Focke-Wulf Fw 190A-3/U1, which, carrying a 1,100 lb (500 kg) bomb, caused even more problems for the British defences. On 31 October, thirty fighter-bombers, escorted by as many fighters, carried out an attack on Canterbury, two Fw 190s being lost. To counter the growing problem of these hit-and-run attacks, RAF Fighter Command formed special interception squadrons, which were based as close as possible to the most severely hit targets and maintaind at a high level of readiness. It was soon apparent, however, that the main line of defence – the Spitfire – was unable to cope with the faster Focke-Wulf Fw 190A-4 with which the *Jabo* units were now equipped.

Only one RAF fighter had the necessary speed to catch the Fw 190, and that was the Hawker Typhoon. A cantilever low-wing monoplane of basically all-metal stressed-skin construction with a retractable tailwheel, the Hawker Typhoon was designed in response to a 1937 Air Staff requirement, leading to Air Ministry Specification F.18/37, for an aircraft capable of taking on heavily armed and armoured escort fighters like the Messerschmitt Bf 110. In fact, two separate designs were submitted, the Type R and the Type N. The Type R was powered by a Rolls-Royce Vulture engine; it flew in prototype form as the Tornado, but was abandoned when production of the Vulture was curtailed. The Type N, named Typhoon, was powered by a 2,100 hp Napier Sabre H-type in-line engine and the first of two prototypes flew for the first time on 24 February 1940. The first production aircraft, however, did not fly until May 1941. Delays in production were blamed on the

The fast, heavily-armed Focke-Wulf Fw 190 posed a serious threat to Britain's air defences, and caused substantial damage to targets on Britain's south coast. (Author's collection)

unreliability of the massive Sabre engine, but there were other problems, including structural failures of the rear fuselage. These had still not been cured when No. 56 Squadron at Duxford was issued with the Typhoon in September 1941, and several pilots were lost. Moreover, although the aircraft was fast and handled well at medium and low altitudes, its performance at high altitude was inferior to that of both the Fw 190 and the Messerschmitt Bf 109F, and its rate of climb was poor. Teething troubles with the type kept the squadron non-operational until the end of May 1942, and at one time there was talk of cancelling the Typhoon programme altogether. It was the enemy fighter-bomber attacks that brought about the aircraft's reprieve.

Early in November 1942, No. 609 Squadron, the second unit to equip with the Typhoon under Wing Commander Roland Beamont, was deployed to Manston in Kent to carry out standing patrols over the coastline between Ramsgate and Dungeness. On 20 January 1943 the Typhoon at last showed what it could do as an interceptor. On

Despite ongoing teething troubles, the Hawker Typhoon was rushed into service to counter the Fw 190 menace. It would find its true role in ground-attack operations. (Flight)

that day twenty-eight enemy fighter-bombers, escorted by single-engined fighters, made a daylight attack on London, causing much damage and many casualties. Little warning had been received of the attack, but as the raiders were making their exit from the target area they were intercepted by the Typhoons of No. 609 Squadron. In the ensuing fight Flying Officer Johnny Baldwin, later to become the top-scoring Typhoon pilot with fifteen victories, destroyed three Bf 109Gs, while four Fw 190s were shot down by other pilots. Several more successes were achieved against the enemy fighter-bombers by No. 609 Squadron in the weeks that followed, and during this period the squadron continued to expand its offensive operations against targets on the Continent. There was no longer any doubt about the aircraft's effectiveness at low level, and 609 Squadron's performance effectively killed a last-ditch attempt by the Engineering Branch of Fighter Command, early in 1943, to have the fighter axed in favour of the American P-47 Thunderbolt. By the end of the year, with the aircraft's technical problems cured and the growing number of Typhoon squadrons – now carrying a pair of 500 lb (225 kg) bombs on their aircraft in addition to the built-in cannon armament – striking hard at the enemy's communications,

The Typhoon proved effective against the Fw 190 hit-and-run raiders. The wreckage of one Fw 190 is seen here in an English wood. (Author's collection)

shipping and airfields, the Typhoon was heading for its place in history as the most potent Allied fighter-bomber of all.

Meanwhile, in December 1942, the *Luftwaffe's* fighter-bomber assets in France had been augmented by the formation of *Schnellkampfgeschwader* 10 (SKG. 10), which came under the orders of the *Angriffsführer England* (Attack Commander England) and which was also equipped with the Fw 190A-4. Until 18 June, 1943, when most of the *Geschwader* was deployed to Italy following the Allied landings in Sicily, its fighter-bombers were extremely active in attacks on southern England. I/SKG. 10 remained operational in the Channel area until June 1944, and saw action against the Allied invasion forces before being withdrawn.

By this time, the effectiveness of the British air defences, especially following the introduction of fast, Griffon-engined versions of the Spitfire and the de Havilland Mosquito night fighter, was such that all German offensive operations over the British Isles were restricted to the cover of darkness. In 1943–4 the *Luftwaffe* mounted frequent intruder operations, using mainly Me 410 and Ju 188 aircraft. The Me 410 *Hornisse* (Hornet) was descended from the Bf 110 via the Me 210, which was not a success. Only 352 were built before production switched to the Me 410 late in 1942. As well as being used in the fast bomber role, the Me 410 was used as a night fighter and a bomber destroyer, being armed with a 50 mm cannon in the latter case. We can see a measure of what they might have achieved, had these aircraft been committed in greater numbers, in one attack on American air bases in East Anglia on 2 April 1944, when intruders destroyed thirteen B-24 Liberators and, in the panic, two more were shot down by their own airfield defences. The Germans lost a single Me 410. By the beginning of 1944, however, further improvements in the British air defences had made it hard for the *Luftwaffe* to penetrate into UK air space at medium and low level. Increased numbers of anti-aircraft guns of all calibres, rocket batteries capable of firing salvoes of 128 missiles, and radar-directed searchlights able to illuminate targets up to 35,000 ft (11,000 m) all contributed to frustrating the attackers, and the fast enemy bombers now began to penetrate at up to 30,000 ft (9,000 m) before diving on their objectives and making a high-speed exit. These new tactics caused problems for the night fighters, since following an enemy aircraft in a dive meant that radar contact was often lost because of ground returns. The answer was to extend the night fighter patrol lines well out to sea; many intruders were trapped and destroyed in this way.

The Messerschmitt Me 410 Hornisse *was a great improvement on the Me 210, and carried out many intruder attacks on the British Isles.*
(Author's collection)

Just how effective the Mosquito night fighter could be was demonstrated during Operation *Steinbock*, the so-called 'Little Blitz' of January–May 1944, which was conducted against the British Isles by all available German bombers in the west. It cost the *Luftwaffe* 329 aircraft, of which 129 were destroyed by Mosquitoes.

CHAPTER FOUR

Carrier Strike

A fortnight before the Franco-German Armistice of June 1940 brought the Battle of France to an end, Italy declared war on France and Britain. When Italy entered the war on 10 June, 1940, she had at her disposal six battleships (only two of which were ready for operations), seven heavy cruisers, twelve light cruisers, fifty-nine destroyers, sixty-seven torpedo boats and 116 submarines. Against this, the British in the eastern Mediterranean had four battleships, nine light cruisers, twenty-one destroyers and six submarines, to which could be added one French battleship, three heavy cruisers, one light cruiser, a destroyer and six submarines. Six more British submarines and a destroyer were at Malta. In the western Mediterranean, the combined Anglo-French naval assets were five battleships (four of them French) one aircraft carrier, four heavy cruisers, seven light cruisers (six of them French) forty-six destroyers (thirty-seven French) and thirty-six submarines (all French).

This strategic picture changed completely with the fall of France in June 1940. Under the terms of the Franco-German Armistice, the French fleet was immobilized in the ports that came under the control of the Vichy government, on the French Mediterranean coast, in North Africa or in France's colonial possessions in the Far East and the Caribbean. At one stroke, the Royal Navy in the Mediterranean was deprived of its powerful ally.

Towards the end of June 1940 a strong Royal Navy squadron assembled at Gibraltar under the command of Vice-Admiral Sir James Somerville. Known as Force H, it consisted of the aircraft carrier *Ark Royal*, newly arrived from Britain, the battleships *Valiant* and *Resolution*, two cruisers and eleven destroyers, together with the battlecruiser *Hood*.

Force H was only a week old when it was called upon to carry out one of the most tragic and melancholy operations in the history of

The aircraft carrier Ark Royal *performed valiant service in the Mediterranean until she was sunk by* U-81 *in November 1941.* (Author's collection)

the Royal Navy: the attempted destruction of the French fleet at Oran and Mers-el-Kebir (Operation Catapult). Admiral Somerville was ordered to sail with his squadron to Oran and to offer an unpleasant ultimatum to the French commander, Admiral Gensoul. If the latter refused to join forces with the British, to sail to the French West Indies with reduced crews or to scuttle his ships, then Somerville had orders to destroy them. On 3 July Captain C.S. Holland, in command of the *Ark Royal*, was sent to Oran to parley with Gensoul, but the French admiral refused even to consider any of the alternatives. Shortly before 18.00 hours the *Valiant*, *Resolution* and *Hood* opened fire, their guns directed by Fairey Swordfish spotter aircraft from the *Ark Royal*, while another flight of Swordfish laid mines in the entrance of the nearby port of Mers-el-Kebir. The heavy shells hit the magazine of the battleship *Bretagne* and she blew up; the *Dunkerque* and *Provence* were badly damaged, and two destroyers were sunk.

As the sun went down, the battleship *Strasbourg* and five destroyers made a dash for safety. They were attacked by the *Ark Royal*'s Swordfish, but in the face of heavy fire and the gathering darkness the pilots' aim was poor and the French warships got away to Toulon. The following morning, the *Ark Royal* launched another strike of torpedo-carrying Swordfish to finish off Gensoul's flagship, the *Dunkerque*, which was aground in Oran harbour. Four torpedoes hit the the auxiliary vessel *Terre Neuve*, which was lying alongside *Dunkerque* with a cargo of depth charges; these exploded and ripped open the battleship's side, putting her out of action. Another French squadron, comprising the battleship *Lorraine*, four cruisers and a number of smaller warships, was at *Alexandria*, where it had been operating under Admiral Cunningham, commanding the British Eastern Mediterranean Fleet, before France's collapse. Here Cunningham managed to arrive at a peaceful settlement with his French opposite number, Admiral Godfroy, and the French warships were deactivated. That still left the new battleships *Jean Bart* and *Richelieu* – which had escaped from Brest before the port was captured by the Germans – in the West African ports of Casablanca and Dakar, and on 8 July a fast motor boat from the carrier *Hermes* entered the harbour of Dakar and dropped depth charges under the *Richelieu*'s stern in an attempt to put her rudder and propellers out of action. But the depth charges failed to explode, and although the battleship was later attacked by Swordfish from the carrier *Hermes* their torpedoes only inflicted light damage. She was attacked again two months later, this time by the *Ark Royal*'s aircraft, during an abortive British attempted landing in Senegal; but once again the air strikes proved ineffective, and this time nine Swordfish and Skuas were shot down.

On 7 July Admiral Cunningham, having dealt with the French squadron in Alexandria, sailed from that port with the twofold intention of providing protection for two convoys carrying supplies from Malta to Alexandria, and also of throwing down a challenge to the Italian navy by operating within sight of the southern coast of Italy. Cunningham's force was split into three; the leading unit (Force A) consisted of five cruisers, the centre (Force B) of the battleship *Warspite* and her destroyer screen, and bringing up the rear was Force C, comprising the aircraft carrier *Eagle*, accompanied by ten destroyers and the veteran battleships *Malaya* and *Royal Sovereign*. The British fleet's air cover consisted of fifteen Swordfish of Nos 813 and 824 Squadrons and three Sea Gladiators of a fighter flight, forming *Eagle*'s air group.

Although it appeared antiquated, the Fairey Swordfish was a very effective torpedo-bomber, and remained in first-line service until the end of the war. (Author's collection)

Early on 8 July a patrolling submarine reported that a strong enemy force, including two battleships, was steaming southwards between Taranto and Benghazi. Reconnaissance Swordfish were launched, and they in turn reported that the enemy warships were following an easterly course, which led Cunningham to believe that they were covering a convoy *en route* to Benghazi. Postponing the departure of the British convoy from Malta, he altered course in order to position himself between the enemy and their base at Taranto. At dawn on 9 July, his fleet having endured five days of air attacks that inflicted little damage, Cunningham was 60 miles (100 km) off the south-west tip of Greece, with the enemy force – two battleships, sixteen cruisers and 32 destroyers – about 175 miles (280 km) ahead of him, in the Ionian Sea. By 11.45 only 100 miles (160 km) separated the two forces, and the *Eagle* launched a strike force of nine Swordfish in an attempt to slow down the enemy force.

They failed to find the main force, which had altered course, but launched their torpedoes through a heavy barrage of fire at an Italian cruiser that was bringing up the rear, missed, and returned to the *Eagle* to refuel and rearm.

At 15.15 Cunningham's advance force of cruisers sighted the enemy, who immediately opened fire on them. Ten minutes later the *Warspite* arrived on the scene and engaged the Italian cruisers with her 15-in guns until they were forced to withdraw under cover of a smoke screen. At 15.45 a second Swordfish strike was flown off, and three minutes after the aircraft had gone the *Warspite* made contact with the Italian flagship *Giulio Cesare* and opened fire on her from a range of 26,000 yards (23.8 km), severely damaging her and reducing her speed to 18 knots. The Italian commander, Admiral Campioni, at once broke off the action and headed for the Italian coast, accompanied by the *Cesare*'s sister ship *Conte di Cavour*, at the same time ordering his destroyer flotillas to attack and lay down smoke. At 16.15 the nine Swordfish, led by Lieutenant-Commander Debenham, arrived in the vicinity of the Italian warships, the pilots striving to identify targets in the dense pall of smoke that now hung over the sea. After a few minutes, Debenham spotted two large warships emerging from the smoke and led his aircraft in to the attack. In fact, the two ships were the cruisers *Trento* and *Bolzano*; they immediately turned away into the smoke once more, throwing down a heavy barrage in the path of the attacking Swordfish as they did so. The torpedoes failed to find their mark, and all the aircraft returned safely to the carrier. They landed at 17.05 in the middle of yet another high-level attack by Italian bombers; fortunately none of the British warships was hit, although both *Eagle* and *Warspite* were shaken by near misses. At 17.30, Cunningham abandoned the chase and set course for Malta, where his ships refuelled and rearmed before returning to Alexandria. Without adequate fighter cover, it would have been suicidal to sail any closer to the Italian coast. The Action off Calabria, as Cunningham's brush with the Italians came to be known, was the first fleet action in which carrier aircraft took part.

In the autumn of 1940, the Italians began to concentrate their heavy naval units at Taranto naval base in southern Italy, to counter the threat from the British Mediterranean Fleet. Taranto had long been regarded as a tempting target for the Fleet Air Arm, but with only the old *Eagle* at Admiral Cunningham's disposal, an attack had been considered impracticable. The deployment of the large, modern aircraft carrier HMS *Illustrious* to the Mediterranean at the

The aircraft carrier HMS Illustrious *had a distinguished war career, which ended in the Pacific when her aircraft took part in the final offensive against Japan in 1945.* (Author's collection)

end of August 1940 changed the picture completely; the plans were revised, and it was decided to mount a strike from the *Illustrious* and the *Eagle* on the night of 21 October, the anniversary of the Battle of Trafalgar. In the meantime, however, a serious fire swept through *Illustrious*'s hangar; some of her aircraft were totally destroyed and others put temporarily out of action, and the strike had to be postponed by three weeks.

Air reconnaissance had revealed that five of the six battleships of the Italian battle fleet were at Taranto, as well as a large force of cruisers and destroyers. The battleships and some of the cruisers were moored in the outer harbour, the Mar Grande, a horseshoe-shaped expanse of fairly shallow water, while the other cruisers and destroyers lay in the inner harbour, the Mar Piccolo. The ships in the outer harbour were protected by torpedo nets and lines of barrage balloons. It was the balloons, perhaps even more than the anti-aircraft batteries, that would present the greatest hazard to the low-flying Swordfish. The date of the attack (Operation Judgment) was fixed for the night of 11 November. Because of defects caused by the many near misses she had suffered in enemy air attacks, the *Eagle* had to be withdrawn from the operation at the last moment; five of her aircraft were transferred to the other carrier.

The *Illustrious* and the fleet sailed from Alexandria on 6 November, and two days later the warships made rendezvous with several military convoys in the Ionian Sea, on their way from Malta to Alexandria and Greece. The concentration of ships was located and attacked by the *Regia Aeronautica* during the next two days, but the attacks were broken up by 806 Squadron's Fulmar fighters, which claimed the destruction of ten enemy aircraft for no loss. At 18.00 on the 11th, with the convoys safely on their way under escort, the *Illustrious*, with a screen of four cruisers and four destroyers, detached herself from the main force and headed for her flying-off position 195 miles (310 km) from Taranto. Twenty-one aircraft were available for the strike: twelve from 815 Squadron, led by Lieutenant-Commander Ken Williamson, and nine from No. 819 under Lieutenant Commander J.W. 'Ginger' Hale. Because of the restricted space available over the target, only six aircraft from each wave were to carry torpedoes; the others were to drop flares to the east of the Mar Grande, silhouetting the warships anchored there, or to dive-bomb the vessels in the Mar Piccolo.

The first wave of Swordfish began taking off at 20.40 and set course in clear weather, climbing to 8,000 ft (2,400 metres) and reaching the enemy coast at 22.20. The Swordfish formation now split in two, the torpedo carriers turning away to make their approach from the west while the flare droppers headed for a point east of the Mar Grande. At 23.00 the torpedo aircraft were in position and began their attack, diving in line astern with engines throttled well back. Williamson, descending to 30 ft (9 metres), passed over the stern of the battleship *Diga di Tarantola* and released his torpedo at the destroyer *Fulmine*; it missed and ran on to explode against the side of a bigger target, the battleship *Conte di Cavour*. Then the Swordfish was hit by AA fire and dropped like a stone into the harbour; Williamson and his observer, Lieutenant N.J. 'Blood' Scarlett, were taken prisoner. Two torpedoes from the remaining Swordfish hit the brand-new battleship *Littorio*; the aircraft all got clear of the target area and set course for the carrier. So did the other six Swordfish, whose bombs had damaged some oil tanks and started a big fire in the seaplane base beside the Mar Piccolo.

The second wave, which had taken off some fifty minutes after the first, had no difficulty in locating Taranto; the whole target area was lit up by searchlights and the glare of fires. There were only eight aircraft in this wave; the ninth had been forced to turn back to the carrier with mechanical trouble. This time, the five torpedo carriers came in from the north. Two of their torpedoes hit the *Littorio* and another the *Caio Duilio*; a fourth narrowly missed the *Vittorio Veneto*. The fifth Swordfish (Lieutenant G.W. Bayley and Lieutenant H.G. Slaughter) was hit and exploded, killing both crew members. By 0300 all the surviving Swordfish had been recovered

Air reconnaissance reveals the devastation at Taranto after the Fleet Air Arm strike, with damaged Italian battleships surrounded by lakes of fuel oil. (Author's collection)

safely, although some had substantial battle damage. Some of the crews who had bombed the vessels in the Mar Piccolo reported that some bombs had failed to explode; one had hit the cruiser *Trento* amidships, only to bounce off into the water, and the same had happened with a hit on the destroyer *Libeccio*. The following day, RAF reconnaissance photographs told the full story of the damage inflicted on the Italian fleet. The mighty *Littorio*, with great gaps torn in her side by three torpedoes, was badly down by the bow and leaking huge quantities of oil; it would take four months to effect repairs. The *Caio Duilio* and the *Conte di Cavour* had taken one hit each; the former had been beached and the latter had settled on the bottom. The *Duilio* was repaired and returned to service after six months; the *Cavour* was later salvaged and moved to Trieste, and she was still there when RAF bombers sank her on 17 February 1945.

It was the first time that a formidable battle fleet had been crippled by carrier aircraft, and the effect on the morale of the Italian navy was shattering. After Taranto, the Italian fleet was permanently on the defensive, and the superiority of the Royal Navy in the

A Fairey Swordfish flies over the fleet carrier HMS Formidable, *which also served in the Mediterranean and northern waters before joining the Pacific Fleet in 1945.* (Author's collection)

Mediterranean was assured. The Italian warships would never again present a serious threat to the security of the British convoys that were passing through the Mediterranean in increasing numbers.

On the other side of the world, the lesson of Taranto was absorbed by a senior naval officer who was also a staunch advocate of naval air power. He was Admiral Isoroku Yamamoto, Commander-in-Chief of the Imperial Japanese Navy.

CHAPTER FIVE

Blenheims to Bremen

I
n the summer of 1941, although the idea was strongly opposed
by the RAF group commanders whose squadrons had suffered
fearful losses in the disastrous daylight raids on the north
German ports in late 1939, the British Air Staff once again began to
consider the possibility of mounting daylight attacks on enemy
targets. These thoughts were influenced by two events in particular:
the German invasion of the Balkans in April 1941 and the assault
on the Soviet Union in June, both of which had led to the transfer
of *Luftwaffe* fighter units from the Channel coast area. The Air Staff
believed that if the enemy could be persuaded to pull fighter units
out of Germany to replace those redeployed from the Channel coast,
then daylight penetration raids into Germany might have a chance
of success. It was decided, therefore, to mount a series of strong and
co-ordinated fighter and bomber attacks on objectives in the area
immediately across the Channel.

These attacks, known as 'Circus' operations, got into their stride
in June 1941 with small numbers of bombers escorted by several
squadrons of fighters carrying out daylight raids on enemy airfields
and supply dumps in France. Most of the bombers involved were
the twin-engined Bristol Blenheims of Bomber Command's No. 2
Group, but heavy bombers were occasionally involved; on 19 July,
for example, four-engined Short Stirlings of No. 7 Squadron, strongly
escorted by Spitfires, bombed targets in the vicinity of Dunkirk.

In the meantime, it had been decided that the 'Circus' operations
were keeping sufficient numbers of enemy fighters pinned down
to enable RAF bombers to make unescorted daylight penetrations
into Germany, and on the last day of June Handley Page Halifax
heavy-bombers of No. 35 Squadron made a daylight attack on Kiel,
all returning to base without loss.

On that day, the Blenheims of No. 2 Group were also standing
by to attack an important target in northern Germany: the port of

A Handley Page Halifax heavy-bomber over the Atlantic port of Brest. The German battlecruisers Scharnorst *and* Gneisenau *are partially visible under a smokescreen.* (Author's collection)

Bremen, or more specifically the shipyards in the harbour area. These yards were responsible for roughly a quarter of Germany's U-boat producion, and at a time when enemy submarines were taking an increasing toll of British shipping in the Atlantic the importance of precision-bombing attacks on such objectives could not be over-emphasized. The problem was that the yards actually producing the submarines were extremely difficult to locate at night, and although several night raids had already been carried out on Bremen there was no evidence that submarine production had been affected in the slightest. To achieve the necessary identification and accuracy an attack would have to be made in broad daylight,and Bremen was one of the most heavily defended targets in Europe, protected by a forest of barrage balloons and anti-aircraft guns of every calibre.

The dangerous and difficult mission was assigned to Nos 105 and 107 Squadrons of No. 2 Group, which was responsible for the operations of the RAF's medium-bomber force. The two squadrons were equipped with the Bristol Blenheim Mk IV. Each Blenheim carried a crew of three: pilot, navigator/bomb aimer and wireless operator/air gunner. The last-named sat in a turret on top of the fuselage, behind two 0.303 in Browning machine guns; there were two more guns in a turret under the nose, operated by the navigator, and the fifth gun, which was fixed and fired forward, was operated by the pilot.

The Blenheims had already made one attempt to reach Bremen, on 28 June, but as they approached the enemy coast the sky ahead had revealed itself to be brilliantly blue, without a trace of cloud cover, and the formation leader – Wing Commander Laurence Petley, commanding No. 107 Squadron – had quite rightly ordered his aircraft to turn back. Petley was an old hand, and knew that if the Blenheims pressed on they would have little chance of survival without cloud to shelter in if they were attacked by fighters; in fact, they would probably not even reach the target.

Now, on the 30th, the Blenheims set out for the target once more, this time led by Wing Commander Hughie Idwal Edwards of No. 105 Squadron. Edwards, an athletic six-footer aged twenty-seven, had been born in Fremantle, Australia, on 1 August 1914, the son of a Welsh immigrant family. After his schooling he had worked in a shipping office, a steady but boring job which he left to join the Australian army as a private in 1934. A few months later he obtained a transfer to the Royal Australian Air Force, and in 1936 he was transferred yet again, this time to the RAF. The beginning

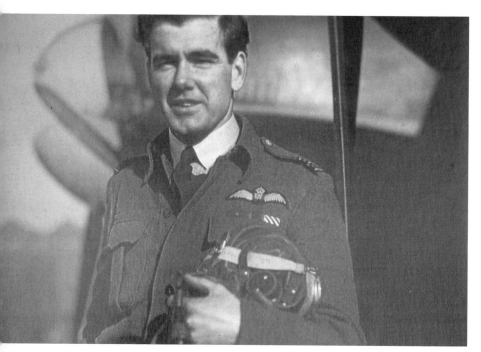

Wing Commander Hughie Edwards, VC, the intrepid low-level ace who led the attack on Bremen. (Author's collection)

of 1938 found him at RAF Station Bicester, flying Blenheim Mk Is with No. 90 Squadron; to be the pilot of what was then Britain's fastest bomber was the fulfilment of all his dreams.

Then, in August 1938, shortly after his twenty-fourth birthday, came disaster. The Blenheim he was flying became caught in severe icing conditions, spinning down out of control through dense cloud. Edwards baled out, but his parachute fouled the aircraft's rudder and he was only a few hundred feet off the ground by the time he managed to free himself. He suffered severe injuries in the resultant heavy landing, the most serious of which was the severing of the main nerve in his right leg, causing paralysis from the knee down.

He spent the next two years in and out of hospital and was told that he would never fly again, but he doggedly refused to accept the fact and in August 1940 he regained his full flying category. He had not long been back with his old squadron at Bicester, however, when bad luck caught him out again. Returning to base after a night-flying exercise on a black, moonless night, he found that an enemy air raid was in progress and all the airfield lighting had been switched off. Unable to land in the pitch darkness, he was forced to fly round in circles until his fuel ran out, whereupon he ordered his crew members to bale out. Then he tried to follow suit, only to find that his escape hatch was jammed, trapping him inside the aircraft. He brought the Blenheim down in a flat glide, flying as slowly as possible, and waited for the impact. A few moments later the bomber slammed through the branches of a tree, hit the ground and broke up, leaving Edwards sitting in the remains of the cockpit with no worse injury than concussion.

The accident, however, delayed the start of his operational career until February 1941, when he flew his first missions with No. 139 Squadron, which was equipped with Blenheims at Horsham St Faith in Norfolk. He at once began to make up for lost time with a series of daring raids, usually at low level, over occupied France. The casualty rate was high, and for those who survived promotion was rapid. It was not long before Edwards was posted to command No. 105 Squadron at the nearby airfield of Swanton Morley with the rank of wing commander, and by the last week of June he had thirty-five operational sorties to his credit.

Edwards had studied the Bremen defences until he knew their layout by heart, and he knew that they could not be penetrated by normal methods. There was only one way to approach and bomb the target, and that was at low level. In this way, with the element of surprise on their side, some of the attacking crews might just stand a chance of getting through. Edwards, however, was under no illusions; operating at very low level meant increased fuel consumption, and even with full tanks the Blenheims would just have enough fuel to make the round trip. If something unforeseen cropped up, such as a strong unexpected headwind on the way back, they might not be able to make it home.

The attempt of 30 June, like that of two days earlier, was doomed to failure. Fifteen Blenheims from the two squadrons took off from Swanton Morley that morning in clear weather conditions, but as they crossed the North sea it was apparent that the weather was deteriorating rapidly. The enemy coast was shrouded in a blanket of dense fog, and although the formation pressed on for several minutes through the grey wall Edwards soon knew that it was hopeless. Only two bombers had managed to keep station with him; the others were scattered in the murk and hopelessly lost. He ordered his wireless operator to tap out the recall signal, and the widely dispersed bombers came straggling back to their Norfolk base.

Early on 4 July the fifteen bombers made a third attempt. Bremen had been bombed on the previous night, and it was hoped that this attack might have caused some disruption of the German defences, giving the Blenheims an extra chance.

The bombers – nine aircraft from No. 105 Squadron and six from No. 107 – assembled over the Norfolk coast and set course in sections of three, flying at 50 ft (15 metres). Edwards' plan was to skirt the shipping lanes near the Friesian Islands and the North German coast, turning in to make a landfall west of Cuxhaven and then making a slight detour to avoid the outer flak defences of Bremerhaven before making a fast, straight-in approach to Bremen.

Edwards was aware that however careful they were, they were certain to be detected by enemy shipping before they reached the coast. Speed and surprise were essential to the attack plan, and as the bombers approached the Freisian Islands their pilots increased speed to a fast cruise of 230 mph (370 kph), sacrificing fuel reserves in a bid to enhance the all-important surprise element. The speed increase proved too much for three of the 107 Squadron aircraft; unable to keep up, they gradually lost contact with the rest of the formation, and their pilots, realizing the folly of continuing, turned for home.

The remaining twelve thundered on, still skimming the surface of the sea. Edwards' navigator, Pilot Officer Ramsay, reported that they were north of Cuxhaven and told the pilot to steer a new heading of 180 degrees, due south towards the mouth of the River Weser. A few moments later, as the Blenheims approached the German coastline, a number of dark shapes suddenly loomed up out of the morning haze. They were merchant ships, and in seconds they had flashed beneath the wings of the speeding bombers. The damage, however, had been done. The ships would already be signalling a warning of the Blenheims' approach – unless, Edwards thought optimistically, the enemy crews had mistaken them for a squadron of Junkers 88s returning from a mission. The Blenheim and the Ju 88 bore a superficial resemblance to one another, and this had often led to confusion in the past, sometimes with fatal results.

The bombers swept over the coast and raced on in a thunderclap of sound over the flat, drab countryside of northern Germany. Edwards had a fleeting glimpse of a horse and cart careering into a ditch in confusion as the Blenheims roared overhead, and of white upturned faces as people in the fields waved at them, mistaking them for German aircraft. In the mid-upper gun turret, the gunner, Flight Sergeant Gerry Quinn, had no eyes for the scenery; he was busy scanning the sky above and to left and right, searching for the first sign of the enemy fighters he was certain must be speeding to intercept them.

Bremerhaven slid by off the bombers' starboard wingtips, a dark smudge under its curtain of industrial haze. A railway line flashed under them, and Edwards picked out the town of Oldenburg away on the right, in the distance. Then, leaning forward in his seat to peer ahead, he picked out a dense cluster of silvery dots, standing out against the blue summer sky. Each one of those dots was a barrage balloon, and in a few more minutes the twelve Blenheims would have to weave their way through the middle of them, into the inferno of the flak barrage that lay beyond.

In order to present more problems to the AA gunners Edwards ordered his pilots to attack in line abreast, with a couple of hundred yards' spacing between each aircraft. The Blenheims of 107 Squadron took up station on the left of the line, with 105 Squadron on the right. The bomber on the extreme left was flown by Wing Commander Petley, who had led the abortive raid of 28 June.

The bombers stuck doggedly to their course as they sped into the forest of barrage balloons. Whether they got through or not was largely a matter of luck; any pilot who took evasive action to miss a cable risked colliding with one of the tall cranes or pylons that cluttered the harbour area. Yet, miraculously, they all did get through, thundering over the drab grey streets, the wharves and the warehouses. All around them now, the sky erupted in fire and steel as the ships around the harbour pumped thousands of shells into their path, and the shellfire began to take its inevitable toll. A Blenheim turned over on its back and crashed into a street, exploding in a wave of burning petrol. A second blew up in mid-air as a shell tore into its bomb bay. A third, one wing torn off, cartwheeled into a group of warehouses, its bombs erupting in a mushroom of smoke and flying masonry.

On the left flank of the formation, Wing Commander Petley's Blenheim suddenly pulled up into a climb, flames streaming from its engines. It turned, as though the pilot was desperately trying to regain control and seek somewhere to land, but a few moments later it plunged vertically into a sports field.

The rest raced on, over streets filled with panic-stricken people who scattered for shelter from the sleet of shrapnel that rained down on them from their own AA guns, a greater menace to individuals than the bombers roaring overhead. Every bomber was hit time after time, shell splinters and bullets ripping through wings and fuselage. Then they darted into the vast, sprawling docks area, each pilot selecting his individual target among the complex of factories, sheds, warehouses and wharves that lay in his path. From this height, it was virtually impossible to miss. The Blenheims lurched and jolted violently in the shock waves as the explosions of their bombs sent columns of debris hurtling hundreds of feet into the air. Clouds of smoke boiled up, obscuring the harbour, as the bombers plunged on through the outer ring of defences, all of them still taking hits.

The worst of the flak was behind them now, but the danger was not yet over. Still flying at 50 ft (15 metres), Edwards was suddenly horrified to see a line of high-tension cables directly in his path. Acting instinctively, he eased the control column forward a fraction and dipped underneath them, the bomber's wingtip scraping past a pylon with only a couple of feet to spare. Seconds later, the Blenheim lurched as it scythed its way through some telegraph wires.

The eight surviving bombers raced for the sanctuary of the coast, skimming over woods and villages. Every aircraft was holed like a sieve, and many of the crew members were wounded. They included Gerry Quinn, Edwards' gunner, who had a shell splinter in his knee. One Blenheim had yards of telephone wire trailing from its tailwheel. All the aircraft returned safely to base, but many of them were so badly damaged that they had to be scrapped.

For his part in leading the attack, Hughie Edwards was awarded the Victoria Cross. his navigator received the Distinguished Flying Cross, and Gerry Quinn a bar to his Distinguished Flying Medal. Members of several other crews were also decorated.

There was no denying that the Bremen raid had been a very gallant effort, with enormous propaganda value at a time when Britain was suffering serious reverses in the Western Desert and the Atlantic, but the damage inflicted on the target hardly justified the fact that 33 per cent of the attacking force had been lost over the target. Taking into account the aircraft that had to be written off later because of battle damage, this figure climbed to 60 per cent.

A Blenheim of No. 114 Squadron makes its escape after the attack on the Knapsack power station, Cologne. Note the flak bursts dotting the sky.
(Author's collection)

Despite this, on 12 August 1941 No. 2 Group launched a low-level daylight attack on the Knapsack and Quadrath power stations near Cologne by 54 Blenheims, each carrying two 500 lb (225 kg) bombs. The bombing was accurate, but ten Blenheims were shot down. On this occasion the bombers were escorted to the target by twin-engined Westland Whirlwinds of No. 263 Squadron, the only fighters with sufficient range. Fighter Command flew a total of 175 sorties in support of the raid, which was the deepest daylight penetration made so far by Bomber Command.

Hughie Edwards did not take part in this mission, having departed for Malta with Nos 105 and 107 Squadrons. He carried out many more dangerous low-level missions, in the Mediterranean theatre and in north-west Europe. Successive appointments before the war ended placed him in command of RAF Station Binbrook in 1943–4 and RAF Chittagong, India, in 1945. He ended the war with the VC, DSO and DFC, retiring as an air commodore in 1963. He was appointed Governor of Western Australia in 1974, and was knighted in that year. He died in Sydney on 5 August, 1982.

CHAPTER SIX

Assault on the Malay Coast

For two days, the monsoon rains had been sweeping across the Malay Peninsula, the water falling in sheets from the clouds that rose in leaden banks from the roof of the jungle. The rains lashed the surface of Kota Bharu airfield into stinking mud and danced in an explosive mist on the tarpaulins that shrouded the engines and cockpit canopies of the thirteen Lockheed Hudson bombers of No. 1 Squadron, Royal Australian Air Force (RAAF), standing squat and silent on the flight line.

No. 1 was one of three RAAF squadrons which had been rushed to Singapore in the summer of 1940 to form part of the air defence of Malaya against the growing threat of Japanese expansion in South-East Asia. Australian defence planners rightly considered that Australia's security depended largely on the maintenance of Singapore as a strong base, and the offer of an air contribution to the Malayan garrison had been readily accepted by the British government. Yet, when Japan signed a ten-year military, political and defensive pact with Germany and Italy – nations with which the British Empire and its Commonwealth were already locked in bitter conflict – on 27 September 1940, the Allied staffs were forced to admit that in the event of a war in the Far East, which now seemed a strong possibility, the ability to hold Malaya beyond the immediate vicinity of Singapore Island was problematical and that the survival of Singapore itself for any length of time could not be guaranteed.

A year later, when war with Japan seemed imminent, No. 1 Squadron had been ordered to its war station at Kota Bharu in north-east Malaya. Its primary duty was general reconnaissance and sea attack, with the bombing of land targets a secondary role.

The Lockheed Hudson patrol bomber, seen here in the markings of No 206 Squadron RAF Coastal Command, performed sterling service with both the RAF and RAAF. (Author's collection)

The squadron had been the first RAAF unit to equip with the American-built Hudson, and the aircrews were well content with it. Modern and relatively fast at 255 mph (400 kph), it could carry 1,400 lb (635 kg) of bombs and was armed with up to seven machine-guns. RAF Coastal Command had already been using the type for two years, with considerable success.

The Japanese had been sending reconnaissance aircraft over the Malay Peninsula since early in October 1941, by which time No. 1 Squadron had begun its own series of reconnaissance flights out to sea, the Hudsons ranging up to 300 miles (500 km) from Kota Bharu. By 1 December, reported Japanese troop movements in southern Indo-China, together with the rapidly deteriorating state of Japanese-American relations, had convinced the British Commander-in-Chief in the Far East, Air Chief Marshal Sir Robert Brooke-Popham, that the moment had come to bring all the forces under his command to full readiness.

It was not before time. On the morning of 6 December, taking advantage of a sudden and unexpected lull in the monsoon, three of No. 1 Squadron's Hudsons took off to carry out a sea search of three different sectors off the north-east coast of Malaya. Two of the aircraft reported nothing; the third, piloted by Flight Lieutenant Ramshaw, encountered what appeared to be half the Imperial Japanese Battle Fleet, 265 miles (425 km) due east of Kota Bharu and apparently heading directly for it.

It was 12.30. Ramshaw identified a battleship, five cruisers, seven destroyers and twenty-two transport vessels and at once radioed for permission to shadow them. This was refused and he reluctantly turned for home, his rear gunner reporting the course of the ships until they vanished behind a curtain of rain.

What Ramshaw had seen, in fact, was not a battleship but the heavy cruiser *Chokai*, flagship of Vice-Admiral Ozawa. There was another cruiser, too, the *Sendai*, and twelve destroyers, not seven. In the prevailing weather conditions, the mistakes were easy enough to make. It did not really matter. What did matter was that the transport vessels – there were in fact eighteen of them – were carrying nearly 27,000 troops of the Imperial Japanese Army's 5th Infantry Division, under the command of Lieutenant-General Matsui, and that the whole force was heading for the coast of Malaya.

During the remainder of that day and most of the next, the Australian crews tried in vain to relocate the Japanese naval force, the Hudsons flying in the most appalling weather conditions. The sea approaches to Malaya were almost completely hidden under a blanket of low cloud, rain and fog. Somewhere beneath that grey curtain were the Japanese. By this time, the Allied staff in Singapore had no doubt that they meant to attempt a landing, but as yet there was no indication as to where that would be. An invasion of Malaya would mean all-out war between Imperial Japan and the British Empire, but a second option was open to the Japanese; it might be their intention to launch a seaborne invasion of Thailand, in which case an outbreak of hostilities with Britain and her Allies might not be inevitable.

The search for the Japanese went on. Late on 6 December, a long-range Catalina flying boat – a civilian machine, flown by an Australian airline crew and pressed into service by the Singapore authorities – also took off to look for the ships. It never returned. The Japanese remained undetected, and in Singapore feverish preparations for war continued on 7 December. It was now thirty

Because of the demands of the Battle of the Atlantic, very few long-range Consolidated Catalina flying boats were available in the Far East when the Japanese attacked. (Author's collection)

hours since Flight Lieutenant Ramshaw had first sighted the naval force, and since then there had been no further reports. At Kota Bharu, frustration was intense. There was simply no way of knowing what the Japanese intended to do, and until they made their move no action could be taken against them. They held all the cards.

Suddenly, just before midnight on 7 December, there was news. Wing Commander Davis – No. 1 Squadron's commanding officer, who was in conference with Army Brigade Intelligence at Kota Bharu – received a report that four small vessels were moving along the coast from north to south, close inshore. Davis at once ordered one of his Hudsons into the air to drop flares and photograph the ships. Shortly afterwards, its crew reported that the vessels had turned sharply away to the north and were heading back up the coast towards Thailand.

The Hudson returned to base. Its arrival was followed by a tension-filled lull that ended abruptly at 13.00, when Japanese transports were seen lying at anchor off the coast and British coastal defence batteries opened fire on them. The escorting Japanese warships replied immediately; the first shots of the war in the Far East had been exchanged, but soon their echoes would be eclipsed by events far to the east, on the other side of the International Date-line. Shortly before the sun rose on what promised to be a beautiful, sunny Sunday morning, the first of 276 bombers and torpedo bombers, escorted by eighty fighters, were beginning to take off from six aircraft carriers of the Japanese First Naval Air Fleet. In a few hours' time they would be sweeping down on an unsuspecting Pearl Harbor, the Hawaiian base of the United States Pacific Fleet.

The gunfire along the coast could be heard clearly on Kota Bharu airfield. Within minutes, Wing Commander Davis received an urgent call from the Army, saying that Japanese vessels were anchored off the coast and that a landing appeared to be imminent. Bluntly, the Army wanted to know whether the RAAF could provide air support while the invaders were repulsed. Davis told Singapore what was happening, and quickly received orders to attack the enemy ships with all available aircraft. Some of the Hudsons were already bombed-up and the first of these, piloted by Flight Lieutenant Lockwood, roared away from Kota Bharu at 01.08 and disappeared into the inky darkness.

Lockwood had no difficulty in finding the scene of the action. The darkness over the coast was split by the flash of gunfire, and drifting flares gave the whole picture a stark, nightmarish quality. Crossing the coast at 2,000 ft (600 metres), Lockwood soon located the Japanese transports. There were three of them; the remainder, it later turned out, had headed northwards to carry out separate landings in Thailand, at Singora and Patani.

Lockwood pushed the Hudson's nose down and streaked over the lurid sea at 50 ft (15 metres), heading for one of the Japanese vessels. AA fire lanced at him from all directions but he held the Hudson steady, releasing two bombs and then jinking away from the streams of tracer. His rear gunner reported columns of water rising close to the ship.

Turning, Lockwood brought his aircraft round for a second attack, curving in to drop his second pair of 250 lb (113 kg) bombs. The fire from the escorting warships was intense and the Hudson was hit again and again, but once more the pilot kept the shuddering aircraft on course and tore through the holocaust before the welcome 'clunk' of the bomb-release gear gave him the signal to twist away to safety. This time, the jubilant rear gunner shouted that both bombs had struck the transport amidships. A column of flame lanced up into the night, then died to a dull red glow as the Hudson sped for home.

The second Hudson to attack was not so lucky. Taking off at 02.18 and piloted by Flight Lieutenant Leighton-Jones of Melbourne, the aircraft was shot down flaming into the sea. Not until much later was it learned that this aircraft had carried out a fiercely determined attack, even when damaged and on fire, and that its bombs had severely damaged a second enemy transport.

The third Hudson to come roaring down out of the night was flown by Flight Lieutenant Ramshaw, who had been the first to sight the invasion fleet. He made his attack without seeing any dramatic result, managed to avoid the worst of the flak and returned to Kota Bharu, where ground crew worked feverishly to rearm his aircraft.

The fourth pilot, Flight Lieutenant O'Brien, who took off at 02.20, made a near-perfect attack approach, selecting the biggest of the three enemy transports. He pressed the bomb release – and nothing happened. Hauling the bomber round he made a second attack, thundering low over the ship and raking its decks with machine-gunfire before jinking away over the sea, pursued by meshes of tracer.

After a lull of fifty minutes, the Australians came back. This time, two Hudsons, flown by Ramshaw and Lockwood, making their second sortie, attacked simultaneously. Lockwood dropped his bombs and got away, but Ramshaw's aircraft never returned. For nearly four years, its fate was to remain a mystery. Then, late in 1945, Ramshaw's navigator, Flying Officer Dowie, came home from a Japanese prison camp and told how the Hudson had been shot into the sea as the pilot made his final bomb run. All on board except Dowie had been killed.

Five minutes later, Flight Lieutenant O'Brien returned for his second attack of the night. He noticed that the enemy transports were now anchored very close inshore and dropped his bombs squarely on one of them, his gunner observing what appeared to be two direct hits. All through O'Brien's attack, his aircraft had to run the gauntlet of intense and very accurate fire from the Japanese cruiser that was supporting the enemy landing, but although the aircraft sustained considerable damage its pilot nursed it back to base.

The fury went on hour after hour, the Australian crews taking off to make fresh attacks as soon as their aircraft were made ready by the toiling ground crews. The aircraft were operating from a single strip which, after weeks of almost continual rain, would normally have been classed unserviceable; amazingly, there were no accidents on take-off or landing. Nevertheless, the battle was taking its toll. Two Hudsons had been shot down, and others returned in a progressively worse state after every sortie. The ground crews worked valiantly to patch them up with whatever materials they could find, but spares were in short supply and in the end two of the more severely damaged bombers were 'cannibalized' to keep the others flying.

Meanwhile, the Japanese infantry had begun landing on the beaches near Kota Bharu at 03.00. Seven thousand miles (11,200 km)

7 December 1941, and the Japanese surprise attack on Pearl Harbor goes in, devastating the naval base and nearby airfields. (Author's collection)

away, in mid-Pacific, American servicemen were either asleep or wending their way back to barracks from Oahu's bars and nightspots. There was still an hour and a quarter to go before the peace of an Hawaiian Sunday morning would be shattered by the bombs of Vice-Admiral Nagumo's carrier aircraft.

The Japanese at Kota Bharu were met by heavy rifle, machine-gun and mortar fire from defensive positions along the beach, manned mostly by Indian troops, and suffered appalling casualties. Nevertheless, the enemy quickly succeeded in breaking through the defences at several points, pushing into the screen of forest that separated Kota Bharu airfield from the beach. On the airfield itself, Wing Commander Davis had no idea how far the enemy landings had succeeded. Communications with the Army had broken down, and confusion was everywhere. Then, shortly after 04.00, ground crews working on the squadron's Hudsons reported that they were coming under fire from rifles and automatic weapons. The Japanese had reached the airfield perimeter.

Despite the added danger, the pace of work never slackened as the surviving Hudsons were refuelled and rearmed one after another. By this time, two of the enemy transports were burning fiercely, and shortly afterwards one of them blew up. She was the 9,749 ton *Awigasan Maru*, and the casualties among the troops still waiting to disembark were fearsome; some accounts later told how 5,000 Japanese died on this one ship alone.

The Australian aircrews now turned their attention to the enemy landing barges, bombing them and strafing the soldiers who were struggling ashore through the surf. It was later confirmed that the aircraft had destroyed at least twenty-four landing craft.

Dawn came, and as its grey light spread across the sea the aircrews began to have a real indication of the havoc their mast-height attacks had wrought during the night. A great pall of smoke rose up to meet the clouds from the shattered wrecks of the two freighters, while the shallows along the whole length of the beach were coloured pink with the blood of Japanese soldiers. The entire shoreline was thick with lifeless corpses, bobbing like driftwood on the tide.

At about 08.00, the hard-pressed crews of No. 1 Squadron received additional support when No. 8 Squadron RAAF, which had moved up to its war station at Kuantan, 150 miles (240 km) down the coast, sent its Hudsons into action against the Japanese at Kota Bharu. During the first days of December this squadron had received six brand-new Bristol Beaufort torpedo bombers, but they were unarmed and their crews had received no operational training, so five of them had been ordered back to Australia straight away. The sixth, still without any armament, was now flown up to Kota Bharu to carry out a reconnaissance mission over southern Thailand. It staggered back almost shot to ribbons after being attacked by enemy fighters, but its crew confirmed that the main Japanese convoy was off Singora and that about sixty Japanese fighters were based on the adjacent airfield.

This was bad news, for Singora was just over 100 miles (160 km) away – easily within the combat radius of Japanese fighters. It was not long before they made their presence felt. At about 09.00, a flight of four Mitsubishi Zero fighters appeared over Kota Bharu and made several firing passes before disappearing to the north; fortunately they caused little damage, but air attacks continued sporadically throughout the morning and made air operations increasingly hazardous.

Sniper fire from the airfield perimeter also continued to be a nuisance, and although the Japanese were being held their bullets took an inevitable toll. To bolster the defensive firepower, the Australians removed machine-guns from unserviceable Hudsons and mounted them on makeshift tripods. Apart from exchanging bursts of fire with the enemy on the perimeter, these weapons were also used as anti-aircraft guns in the hope that they might discourage at least some of the low-flying Japanese fighters. In this, they failed.

The battle of the barges went on, the Hudsons now attacking enemy craft on the Kelantan river. At 11.00 the crews reported that the Japanese warships which had supported the invasion appeared to be withdrawing; if a strong force of Allied troops had been available to go into action at this point, the Japanese would probably have been wiped out. But no such force existed.

By midday on 8 December, No. 1 Squadron had only five airworthy Hudsons left out of its original thirteen. Desperate hand-to-hand fighting was now going on in the airfield's domestic site between the Japanese and a dwindling band of gallant Indian troops, and enemy snipers had now moved up to within 200 yards of where the ground crews were working on the surviving aircraft. The airmen sheltered as best they could behind wrecked aircraft and got on with their task, but there was no real cover and at 14.00 Wing Commander Davis decided that the airfield would have to be evacuated.

Air and ground crews had now been operating non-stop in appalling conditions for nearly fourteen hours, and the men were exhausted. They would not know the facts until much later, but their efforts had come close to turning the Japanese invasion at Kota Bharu into a disaster. The air attacks, coupled with the gallant defence on the ground, had inflicted a staggering 15,000 casualties on the enemy.

Now it was over – or rather, just beginning. At 14.30, the five serviceable Hudsons, each carrying two crews and as many airmen and equipment as they could pack in, took off under fire and flew to Kuantan. The remainder of the personnel left by road at 18.15. One man who should have been with them was Flight Lieutenant Jack Douglas, whose Hudson had been badly shot up during an attack on the Japanese cruiser earlier in the day. The ground crews had not had time to repair it, and so Douglas had orders to destroy it.

But he was an unusually determined man. The Hudson's hydraulics had been shot to bits and the wing flaps were dangling uselessly, but the pilot grabbed a handful of wire and tied them in the 'up' position while enemy bullets crackled around his ears. Jumping into the cockpit, he managed to get the engines started and began to taxi towards the runway with Japanese soldiers running after him and taking pot-shots. Pausing only to pick up nine airmen who had been setting fire to damaged aircraft, he opened the throttles and somehow got the bullet-riddled machine into the air. He made the trip to Kuantan with his undercarriage down and the Hudson threatening to shake itself apart, eventually making a safe landing in almost total darkness.

Meanwhile, events were about to unfold that would rock the British nation to its foundations. In the early 1920s, the Government had decided to build a strong naval base in the Far East in the hope of ensuring that an increasingly powerful Japan would be deterred from threatening important British political and economic interests in South-East Asia, Australasia and India. The choice of Singapore was based on the backward-looking assumption that naval power would be the key; in other words, that a battle fleet based on Singapore would be sufficient to deter and if necessary repel attack.

In the two decades that followed, several strategic factors came to be appreciated. First, it was unlikely that a large naval force could in reality be spared from elsewhere and get there in time; secondly, an attack was more likely to come overland from the north than via seaborne assault, which meant that the key to Singapore's strength lay in the defence of the Malayan approaches; and thirdly, any successful defence of Malaya and Singapore would be impossible without the presence of a substantial air force. All three factors were appreciated as early as 1937 by the military authorities on the spot, who were convinced that the best way for the Japanese to attack would be to use Indo-China as the base for landings in Thailand and north-east Malaya and then advance south.

The Admiralty's plan to reinforce the Indian Ocean theatre with warships drawn from the Mediterranean Fleet, leaving the French navy to concentrate on the Mediterranean, was dislocated by the collapse of France in 1940. In August 1941, another Admiralty plan envisaged reinforcing the Far East with six capital ships, a modern aircraft carrier and supporting light forces by the spring of 1942; in the meantime, the best that could be done was to send out the new battleship *Prince of Wales*, supported by the old battlecruiser *Repulse* (which had been launched in 1916) and the aircraft carrier *Indomitable*, which was to provide the essential air component. Even this plan was disrupted when the *Indomitable* ran aground off Jamaica while she was working up there; it was another fortnight before she was ready to sail.

The *Prince of Wales*, meanwhile, flagship of Rear-Admiral Sir Tom Phillips, had sailed from the Clyde on 25 October accompanied by the destroyers *Electra* and *Express*, under orders to proceed to Singapore via Freetown, Simonstown and Ceylon, where they were joined on 28 November by the *Repulse* from the Atlantic and the destroyers *Encounter* and *Jupiter* from the Mediterranean. The force reached Singapore on 2 December.

The Admiralty had always been reluctant to concentrate its warships on Singapore, preferring to base them further back on Ceylon; the fact that they were there at all was at the insistence of Winston Churchill, whose view – supported by the Foreign Office – was that their presence would be enough to deter the Japanese from taking aggressive action. There were justifiable fears, in view of the *Indomitable*'s absence, of the force's vulnerability to enemy air attack. The RAF's air defences on Singapore and the Malay peninsula were woefully weak: about eighty American-built Brewster Buffalo fighters equipped four squadrons, two RAAF, one RAF and one Royal New Zealand Air Force (RNZAF). All four squadrons had been formed within the last eight months, many of their pilots were inexperienced, and their aircraft – heavy, underpowered and underarmed – were wholly outclassed by the Japanese fighters they would soon encounter.

Not long before Admiral Phillips took up his new command (he had been Vice-Chief of Naval Staff) a friend made a cautionary remark to him. 'Tom, you've never believed in air. Never get out from under the air umbrella; if you do, you'll be for it.' They were prophetic words, and the man who made them was Air Marshal Sir Arthur Harris, soon to be appointed Air Officer Commander-in-Chief Bomber Command.

Anxiety over the exposed position of Phillips' ships led the Admiralty to urge him to take them away from Singapore, and on 5 December 1941 the *Repulse*, under Captain Tennant, sailed for Port Darwin in northern Australia. The next day, however, a Japanese convoy was reported off Indo-China, and Tennant was ordered back to Singapore to rejoin the flagship. Only hours later came the news of the Japanese attack on the US Pacific Fleet at Pearl Harbor, with simultaneous amphibious assaults elsewhere, including Malaya and Thailand, and on the evening of 8 December Admiral Phillips took the *Prince of Wales*, *Repulse* and four destroyers, collectively known as Force Z, to attack the Japanese amphibious forces which had landed at Singora.

Early the next morning Singapore advised him that no fighter cover would be available and that strong Japanese bomber forces were reported to be assembling in Thailand, and this, together with the knowledge that his warships had been sighted by enemy reconnaissance aircraft, persuaded Phillips to abandon his sortie at 20.15 on 9 December, reversing course for Singapore. (In fact Force Z had also been sighted by the submarine I-65, but the position it transmitted was inaccurate, and other enemy submarines failed to detect the ships at this time.)

Just before midnight, Phillips received a signal that the Japanese were landing at Kuantan and he turned towards the coast, intending to intercept this new invasion force. The report was false, but in the early hours of 10 December Force Z was sighted by the submarine I-58. Its captain, Lieutenant-Commander Kitamura, made an unsuccessful torpedo attack, then shadowed the British ships for five and a half hours, sending regular position reports that enabled reconnaissance aircraft of the twenty-second Naval Air Flotilla to sight them and maintain contact. Already airborne from airfields in Indo-China were twenty-seven bombers and sixty-one torpedo aircraft, the flotilla's attack element, flying steadily south. They passed to the east of Force Z and flew on for a considerable distance before turning, and at about 11.00 they sighted the ships.

The air attacks were executed with great skill and co-ordination, the high-level bombers – Mitsubishi G4M1s – running in at 12,000 ft (3,600 metres) to distract the attention of the warships' AA gunners while the torpedo bombers, G3M2s, initiated their torpedo runs from different directions. Two torpedo hits were quickly registered on the *Prince of Wales*, severely damaging her propellers and steering gear and putting many of her AA guns out of action. For some time the *Repulse*, by skilful evasive action, managed to avoid the attackers; but there were too many aircraft, and eventually she was hit by four torpedoes. At 12.33 she rolled over and sank, and fifty minutes later the same fate overtook the flagship, which had meanwhile sustained two more torpedo hits. The accompanying destroyers picked up 2,081 officers and men; 840 were lost, among them Admiral Phillips and Captain Leach of the *Prince of Wales*. Captain Tennant of the Repulse survived, having been literally pushed off the bridge by his officers at the last moment.

No one in Singapore could understand the failure of Admiral Phillips to break radio silence, even when he knew his vessels had been sighted by the enemy, and call for help. It was only an hour and a half later, when the ships had been under air attack for three quarters of an hour, that a signal was sent to inform Singapore what was happening, and even then it was Captain Tennant, not Phillips, who sent it. Eleven Buffaloes of No. 453 Squadron RAAF were immediately despatched and arrived in the area ninety minutes later, long after the Japanese had departed.

In Singapore, the news of the sinking of the warships was greeted with disbelief. Nevertheless, there were few who seriously thought that the Japanese, now advancing down the Malay peninsula, would get anywhere near the Johore Strait, which separated Singapore island from the mainland. And as for the notion that Singapore itself might fall – well, that was ridiculous. Everyone knew that the fortress was impregnable.

Its supplies and garrison exhausted, it capitulated to the Japanese on Sunday, 15 February 1942.

CHAPTER SEVEN

By Daylight to Augsburg

On 17 April 1942, RAF Bomber Command mounted one of the most audacious missions of the Second World War. The target was the Maschinenfabrik Augsburg-Nürnberg (MAN) diesel engine factory at Augsburg in Bavaria, which was responsible for the production of roughly half Germany's output of U-boat engines. The Augsburg raid, apart from being one of the most daring and heroic ever undertaken by Bomber Command, was notable for two main things: it was the longest low-level penetration made during the war, and it was the first mission flown by the command's new Lancaster bombers in the teeth of strong enemy opposition.

The prototype Avro Lancaster had been delivered to the RAF for operational trials with No. 44 Squadron at Waddington, near Lincoln, in September 1941. On 24 December it was followed by three production Lancaster Mk Is, and the nucleus of the RAF's first Lancaster squadron was formed. In January 1942 the new bomber also began to replace the Avro Manchesters of No. 97 Squadron at Coningsby, another Lincolnshire airfield.

Four aircraft of No. 44 Squadron carried out the Lancaster's first operation on 3 March 1942, laying mines in the German Bight, and the first night bombing mission was flown on 10 March when two aircraft of the same squadron took part in a raid on Essen. In all, fifty-nine squadrons of Bomber Command were destined to equip with the Lancaster before the end of the war, and this excellent aircraft was to become the sharp edge of the RAF's sword in the air offensive against Germany. Developed from the twin-engined Manchester, whose Rolls-Royce Vulture engines were disastrously unreliable, the Lancaster was powered by four Rolls-Royce Merlins,

The Avro Lancaster, seen here in the markings of No 44 (Rhodesia) Squadron, brought a whole new dimension to Bomber Command's striking power.
(Author's collection)

the splendid engines that also powered Fighter Command's Spitfires and Hurricanes. It carried a crew of seven and had a defensive armament of ten 0.303-in Browning machine-guns. It had a top speed of 287 mph (460 kph) at 11,500 ft (3,500 metres) and could carry a normal bomb load of 14,000 lb (6.350 kg) – although later versions could lift the massive 22,000 lb (10,000 kg) 'Grand Slam' bomb, used to attack hardened targets in the last months of the war.

Because of the growing success of Hitler's U-boats in the Atlantic, the MAN factories at Augsburg had long been high on the list of priority targets. The problem was that getting there and back involved a round trip of 1,250 miles (2,000 km) over enemy territory, and the factories covered a relatively small area. With the navigation and bombing aids available earlier, the chances of a night attack pinpointing and destroying such an objective were very remote, and a daylight precision attack, going on past experience, would be prohibitively costly.

Then the Lancaster came along, and the idea of a deep-penetration precision attack in daylight was resurrected. With its relatively high speed and strong defensive armament, it was possible that a force of Lancasters might get through to Augsburg if they went in at low level, underneath the German warning radar. Also, a Lancaster flying 'on the deck' could not be subjected to attacks from below, its vulnerable spot. A lot would depend, too, on the route to the target. RAF Intelligence had compiled a reasonably accurate picture of the disposition of German fighter units in western Europe, which early in 1942 were seriously overstretched. Half the total German fighter force was deployed in Russia and another quarter in the Balkans and North Africa; most of the remaining squadrons, apart from those earmarked for the defence of Germany itself, were stationed in the Pas de Calais area and Norway. The danger point was the coast of France; if the Lancasters could slip through a weak spot, perhaps in conjunction with a strong diversionary attack, then the biggest danger, in theory at least, would be behind them.

Although Bomber Command's new chief, Air Marshal Arthur Harris, was generally opposed to small precision raids, being a strong advocate of large-scale 'area' attacks on enemy cities, the situation in the North Atlantic, with its awful daily toll of Allied shipping, compelled him to authorize the Augsburg plan. If it succeeded, it might reduce the number of operational U-boats for some time to come, and at the same time silence those in high places who were clamouring for RAF Bomber Command to divert more of its resources to hunting them.

The operation was to be carried out by six crews from No. 44 Squadron at Waddington and six from No. 97, now at Woodhall Spa in Lincolnshire, the two most experienced Lancaster units. A seventh crew from each squadron would train with the others, to be held in reserve in case anything went wrong at the last minute.

For three days, starting on 14 April 1942, the two squadrons practised formation flying at low level, making 1,000 mile (1,600 km) flights around Britain and carrying out simulated attacks on targets in northern Scotland. It was exhausting work, hauling thirty tons of bomber around the sky at such an altitude and having to concentrate on not flying into a neighbouring aircraft as well as obstacles on the ground, but the crews were all very experienced, most of them going through their second tour of operations, and they achieved a high standard of accuracy in the short time available.

Speculation ran high about the nature of the target. To most of the crews, a low-level mission signified an attack on enemy warships, a long, straight run into a nightmare of flak. When they eventually filed into their briefing rooms early on 17 April, and saw the long red ribbon of their track stretching to Augsburg, a stunned silence descended on them. Almost automatically, they registered the details passed to them by the briefing officers. The six aircraft from each squadron were to fly in two sections of three, each section leaving the rendezvous point at a predetermined time. The interval between each section would be only a matter of seconds; visual contact had to be maintained so that the sections could lend support to one another in the event that they were attacked by enemy fighters.

From the departure point, Selsey Bill, the Lancasters were to cross the Channel at low level and make landfall at Dives-sur-Mer, on the French coast. Shortly before this, bombers of No. 2 group, covered by a massive fighter 'umbrella', were to make a series of diversionary attacks on *Luftwaffe* airfields in the Pas de Calais, Rouen and Cherbourg areas. The Lancasters' track would take them across enemy territory via Ludwigshafen, where they would cross the Rhine, to the northern tip of the Ammer See, a large lake some 20 miles (30 km) west of Munich and about the same distance south of Augsburg. By keeping to this route, it was hoped that the enemy would think that Munich was the target. Only when they reached the Ammer See would the bombers sweep sharply northwards for the final run to their true objective.

As they approached the target, the bombers were to spread out so that there was a 3 mile (5 km) gap between each section. Sections would bomb from low level in formation, each Lancaster dropping a salvo of four 1,000 lb (454 kg) bombs. These would be fitted with eleven-second delayed-action fuzes, giving the bombers time to get clear but exploding well before the next section arrived over the target. Take-off was to be in mid-afternoon, which meant that the first Lancasters should reach the target at 20.15, just before dusk. They would therefore have the shelter of darkness by the time they reached the Channel coast danger-areas on the homeward flight. The fuel tanks of each aircraft would be filled to their maximum capacity of 2,154 gal (9,792 litres).

The Lancasters of No. 44 Squadron would form the first two sections. This unit was known as the 'Rhodesia' Squadron, with good reason: about a quarter of its personnel came from that country. There were also a number of South Africans, and one of them was chosen to lead the mission. He was Squadron Leader John Dering Nettleton, a tall, dark 25-year-old who had already shown himself to be a highly competent commander, rock-steady in an emergency. The war against the U-boat was of special interest to him, for after leaving school in Natal he had spent two years in the Merchant Navy and consequently had a fair idea of the agonies seamen went through when their ships were torpedoed. He came from a naval background, too: his grandfather had been an admiral in the Royal Navy. John Nettleton joined the Royal Air Force in 1938, and in April 1942 he was still completing his first operational tour. It was one of the penalties of being an above-average pilot: such men were often 'creamed off' to teach others.

Shortly after 15.00 on 7 April, the quiet Lincolnshire village of Waddington was shaken by the roar of twenty-four Rolls-Royce Merlins as No. 44 Squadron's six Lancasters took off and headed south for Selsey Bill, the promontory of land jutting out into the Channel between Portsmouth and Bognor Regis. Ten miles (15 km) due east, the six bombers of No. 97 Squadron, led by Squadron leader J.S. Sherwood DFC, were also taking off from Woodhall Spa.

Each section left Selsey Bill right on schedule, the sea blurring under the Lancasters as they sped on. The bombers to left and right of Nettleton were piloted by Flying Officer John Garwell and Warrant Officer G.T. Rhodes; the Lancasters in the following section were flown by Flight Lieutenant N. Sandford, Warrant Officer H.V. Crum and Warrant Officer J.E. Beckett. The sky was brilliantly clear and the hot afternoon sun beat down through the perspex of cockpits and gun turrets. Before they reached the coast, most of the crews were flying in shirt sleeves.

As they raced over the French coast the pilots had to ease back their control columns to leapfrog the cliffs, so low were the bombers. They thundered inland across the picturesque landscape of Normandy, the broad loops of the River Seine glistening in the sunshine away to the left. The bombers would pass to the south of Paris and on to Sens, on the Yonne River, their first major checkpoint. Sens lay about 180 miles (290 km) from the Channel coast – about an hour's flying time, at the ground speed the Lancasters were making. If they survived that first hour, if the diversionary raids had drawn off the German fighters, then they would have a good chance of reaching Augsburg.

The bombers were flying over wooded, hilly country near Breteuil when the flak hit them. Lines of tracer from concealed gun positions met the speeding Lancasters, and the ugly black stains of shellbursts dotted the sky around them. Shrapnel ripped into two of the aircraft, but they held their course. The most serious damage was to Warrant Officer Beckett's machine, which had its rear gun turret put out of action.

It was sheer bad luck that drew the German fighters to the Lancasters. The Messerschmitt Bf 109s of II/*Jagdgeschwader* 2 '*Richthofen*' were returning to their base at Evreux after sweeping the area to the south of Paris in search of No. 2 Group's diversionary bombers when they passed directly over the Lancasters' track, actually passing between Nettleton's and Sherwood's formations, although at a much higher altitude. Even then, the bombers might have escaped detection had it not been for a solitary Messerschmitt 109, much lower than the rest, making an approach to land at Evreux with wheels and flaps down.

The German pilot spotted the Lancasters and immediately whipped up his flaps and landing gear, climbing hard and turning in behind Sandford's section. He must have alerted the other fighters, because a few seconds later they came tumbling like an avalanche on the bombers.

The first 109 came streaking in, the pilot singling out Warrant Officer Crum's Lancaster for his first firing pass. Bullets tore through the cockpit canopy, showering Crum and his navigator, Rhodesian Alan Dedman, with razor-sharp slivers of perspex. Dedman looked across at the pilot and saw blood streaming down his face, but when he went to help Crum just grinned and waved him away. The Lancaster's own guns hammered, there was a fleeting glimpse of the 109's pale-grey, oil-streaked belly as it flashed overhead, and then it was gone.

Messerschmitt Bf 109s. Nettleton's crews were unlucky to encounter a large number of these fighters en route *to Augsburg.* (Author's collection)

The Lancasters closed up into even tighter formation as thirty more Messerschmitts pounced on them, and a running fight developed. The Lancaster pilots held their course doggedly; at this height there was no room to take evasive action and they had to rely on the bombers' combined firepower to keep the Germans at bay. It was the first time that *Luftwaffe* fighters had encountered Lancasters, and to begin with the enemy pilots showed a certain amount of caution until they got the measure of the new bomber's defences. As soon as they realized that its defensive armament consisted of 0.303 in machine-guns, however, they began to press home their attacks skilfully, coming in from the port quarter and opening fire with their cannon at about 700 yards (640 m). At 400 yards (366 m), the limit of the .303's effective range, they broke away and climbed to repeat the process.

The Lancasters were raked time after time as they thundered on, their vibrating fuselages a nightmare of noise as cannon shells punched into them and the gunners returned the enemy fire, their pilots drenched with sweat as they dragged the bombers over telegraph wires, steeples and rooftops. In the villages below, people fled for cover as the battle swept over their heads and shells from their own fighters spattered the walls of houses.

Warrant Officer Beckett was the first to go. A great ball of orange flame ballooned from his Lancaster as cannon shells found a fuel tank. Seconds later, the bomber was a mass of fire. Slowly, the nose went down. Spewing burning fragments, the shattered bomber hit a clump of trees and disintegrated.

Warrant Officer Crum's Lancaster, its wings and fuselage ripped and torn, came under attack by three enemy fighters. Both the mid-upper and rear gunners were wounded, and now the port wing fuel tank burst into flames. The bomber wallowed on, almost out of control. Crum, half-blinded by the blood streaming from his face wounds, fought to hold the wings level and ordered Alan Dedman to jettison the bombs, which had not yet been armed. The 1,000- pounders dropped away, and a few moments later Crum managed to put the crippled aircraft down on her belly. The Lancaster tore across a wheatfield and slewed to a stop on the far side. The crew, badly shaken and bruised but otherwise unhurt, broke all records in getting out of the wreck, convinced that it was about to explode in flames. But the fire in the wing went out, so Crum used an axe from the bomber's escape kit to make holes in the fuel tanks and threw a match into the resulting pool of petrol. Within a couple of minutes the aircraft was burning fiercely; there would only be a very charred carcase left for the *Luftwaffe* experts to examine.

Afterwards, Crum and his crew split up into pairs and set out to walk through occupied France to Bordeaux, where they knew they could make contact with members of the French Resistance. All of them, however, were subsequently rounded up by the Germans and spent the rest of the war as prisoners.

Now only Flight Lieutenant Sandford was left out of the three Lancasters of the second section. A quiet music-lover who amused his colleagues because he always wore pyjamas under his flying suit for luck, he was one of the most popular officers on No. 44 Squadron. Now his luck had run out, and he was fighting desperately for his life. In a bid to escape from a swarm of Messerschmitts, he eased his great bomber down underneath some high-tensions cables. The Lancaster dug a wingtip into the ground, cartwheeled and exploded, killing all the crew.

The enemy fighters now latched on to Warrant Officer Rhodes, flying to the right of and some distance behind John Nettleton. Soon, the Lancaster was streaming fire from all four engines. Rhodes must have opened his throttles wide in a last attempt to draw clear, because his aircraft suddenly shot ahead of Nettleton's. Then it went into a steep climb and seemed to hang on its churning propellers for a long moment before flicking sharply over and diving into the ground. There was no chance of survival for any of the crew.

The Lancaster was shot down by another warrant officer, a man named Pohl. Poor Rhodes was the thousandth victim to be claimed since September 1939 by the pilots of JG 2, and a party was held in Pohl's honour at Evreux that night.

There were only two Lancasters left out of the 44 Squadron formation now: those flown by Nettleton and his number two, John Garwell. Both aircraft were badly shot up and their fuel tanks were holed, but the self-sealing 'skins' seemed to be preventing leakage on a large scale. Nevertheless, the fighters were still coming at them like angry hornets, and the life expectancy of both crews was now measured in minutes.

Then the miracle happened. Suddenly, singly or in pairs, the fighters broke off their attacks and turned away, probably running out of fuel or ammunition, or both. Whatever the reason, their abrupt withdrawal meant that Nettleton and Garwell were spared, if only for the time being. They still had more than 500 miles (800 km) to go before they reached the target. Behind them, and a little way to the south, Squadron Leader Sherwood's 97 Squadron formation had been luckier; they never saw the German fighters, and flew on unmolested.

Flying almost wingtip to wingtip, Nettleton and Garwell swept on in their battle-scarred aircraft. There was no further enemy opposition, and the two pilots were free to concentrate on handling their bombers – a task that grew more difficult when, two hours later, they penetrated the mountainous country of southern Germany and had to fly through turbulent air currents that boiled up from the slopes. They reached the Ammer See and turned north, rising a few hundred feet to clear some hills and then dropping down once more into the valley on the other side. And there, dead ahead under a thin veil of haze, was Augsburg.

As they reached the outskirts of the town, a curtain of flak burst across the sky in their path. Shrapnel pummelled their wings and fuselages but the pilots held their course, following the line of the river to find their target. The models, photographs and drawings they had studied at the briefing had been astonishingly accurate and they had no difficulty in locating their primary objective, a T-shaped shed where the U-boat engines were manufactured.

With bomb doors open, and light flak hitting the Lancasters all the time, they thundered over the last few hundred yards. Then the bombers jumped as the 8,000 lb (3,600 kg) of bombs fell from their bellies. The Lancasters were already over the northern suburbs of Augsburg when the bombs exploded, and the gunners reported seeing fountains of smoke and debris bursting high into the evening sky above the target.

Nettleton and Garwell had battled their way through appalling odds and successfully accomplished their mission, but the flak was still bursting around them and now John Garwell found himself in trouble. A flak shell turned the interior of the fuselage into a roaring inferno and Garwell knew that this, together with the severe damage the bomber had already sustained, might lead to her breaking up at any moment. There was no time to gain height so that the crew could bale out; he had to put her down as quickly as possible. Blinded by the smoke that was now pouring into the cockpit, Garwell eased the Lancaster gently down towards what he hoped was open ground. He was completely unable to see anything; all he could do was try to hold the bomber steady as she sank.

A long, agonizing minute later the Lancaster hit the ground, sending earth flying in all directions as she skidded across a field. Then she slid to a stop and Garwell, with three other members of his crew, scrambled thankfully out of the raging heat and choking, fuel-fed smoke into the fresh air. Two other crew members were trapped in the burning fuselage and a third, Sergeant R.J. Flux, had been thrown out on impact. He had wrenched open the ecape hatch just before the bomber touched down; his action had given the others a few precious extra seconds in which to get clear, but it had cost Flux his life.

Completely alone now, John Nettleton set course north-westwards for home, chasing the afterglow of the setting sun. As he did so, the leading section of No. 97 Squadron descended on Augsburg. They had to fly through a flak barrage even more intense than the storm that had greeted Nettleton and Garwell; as well as four-barrelled 20 mm *Flakvierling* cannon, the Germans were using 88 mm guns, their barrels depressed to the minimum and their shells doing far more damage to the buildings of Augsburg than to the racing bombers. All three Lancasters released their loads on the target and thundered on towards safety, their gunners spraying any AA position they could see. The bombers were so low that on occasions they dropped below the level of the rooftops, finding some shelter from the murderous flak.

Sherwood's aircraft, probably hit by a large-calibre shell, began to stream white vapour from a fuel tank. A few moments later flames erupted from it and it went down out of control, a mass of fire, to explode just outside the town. Sherwood alone was thrown clear and survived. The other two pilots, Flying Officers Rodley and Hallows, returned safely with their crews.

The second section consisted of Flight Lieutenant Penman, Flying Officer Deverill and Warrant Officer Mycock. All three pilots saw Sherwood go down as they roared over Augsburg in the gathering dusk. The sky above the town was a mass of vivid light as the enemy gunners hurled every imaginable kind of flak shell into the Lancasters' path. Mycock's aircraft was quickly hit and set on fire but the pilot held doggedly to his course. By the time he reached the target his Lancaster was little more than a plunging sheet of flame, but Mycock held on long enough to release his bombs. Then the Lancaster exploded, its burning wreckage cascading into the streets.

Deverill's Lancaster was also badly hit and its starboard inner engine set on fire, but the crew managed to extinguish the blaze after bombing the target and flew back to base on three engines, accompanied by Penman's Lancaster. Both crews expected to be attacked by night fighters on the home run, but the flight was completely uneventful. It was just as well, for every gun turret on both Lancasters was jammed.

For his part in leading the Augsburg raid, John Nettleton was awarded the Victoria Cross. He was promoted to the rank of wing commander, and the following year saw him flying his second tour of operations. He was killed on the night of 12/13 July 1943, his bomber falling in flames from the night sky over Turin, Italy.

Altough reconnaissance later showed that the MAN assembly shop had been damaged, the full results of the raid were not known until after the war. It appeared that five of the delayed-action bombs which the Lancaster crews had braved such dangers to place on the factory had failed to explode. The others caused severe damage to two buildings, one a forging shop and the other a machine-tool store, but the machine-tools themselves suffered only light damage. The total effect on production was negligible, especially as the MAN had five other factories building U-boat engines at the time.

The loss of seven Lancasters and forty-nine young men was too high a price to pay. Not until the closing months of 1944 would the RAF's four-engined heavy bombers again venture over Germany in daylight, and by then the Allied fighters ruled the enemy sky.

CHAPTER EIGHT

Target Tokyo

On 26 November, 1941, a Japanese striking force, comprising six aircraft carriers and a strong escort that included the former Kongo-class battlecruisers *Hiei* and *Kirishima*, now reclassified as battleships following reconstruction in the late 1930s, left its assembly area at Hittokappu Bay and headed out into the Pacific. Eleven days later, on 7 December, nearly 300 bombers, dive-bombers and torpedo-bombers from the carriers, attacking in two waves, swept down on Pearl Harbor, Hawaiian base of the US Pacific Fleet. The pride of the Pacific Fleet and flagship of Rear-Admiral Isaac C. Kidd, the battleship *Arizona*, hit by a torpedo and eight bombs, exploded and sank with the loss of 1,404 lives. The *California*, severely damaged by bombs and with ninety-eight of her crew dead, sank three days later. The *Nevada*, severely damaged by a torpedo and five bombs that left fifty dead, was beached. The *Oklahoma*, hit by five torpedoes, capsized; 415 of her crew perished. The *West Virginia* sank at her moorings with 105 dead after being torpedoed; and the *Maryland*, *Pennsylvania* and *Tennessee* were heavily damaged. Pearl Harbor, a 'day of infamy' to the Americans, was a master stroke of planning and execution. Its architect was Admiral Isoroku Yamamoto, Commander-in-Chief (C-in-C) of the Japanese Navy, one of the ablest naval commanders of all time, and one on whom the lesson of the British air attack on the Italian fleet at Taranto just over a year earlier had not been lost.

The destruction of the American capital ships left the way open for rapid Japanese conquest in the Pacific, and the weeks that followed the attack on Pearl Harbor saw the new Anglo-American-Australian-Dutch alliance suffer one reverse after another at the hands of the advancing enemy. Malaya, Hong Kong and Singapore fell; gallant but hopeless rearguard actions were fought in the Netherlands East Indies and the Philippines; and in Burma, Allied forces had begun the long retreat towards the Indian frontier. The appalling succession of disasters produced a numbing effect on the morale of the Western powers. The Dutch had seen their homeland overrun in May 1940; now their vital colonies were gone too. The British, reeling under the onslaught of Germany's U-boats at sea and Rommel's Afrika Korps in the Western Desert, now underwent the agony of seeing their 'impregnable' fortress of Singapore topple like a ripe plum, with almost ridiculous ease, into the hands of Imperial Japan.

But it was America, once the shock of Pearl Harbor had given way to a rising tide of anger and determination, which took the initiative in forming a plan that was to give the Allied peoples, military and civilian alike, a much needed shot in the arm at a time when morale had plunged almost to rock bottom. It was a plan which, in its execution, would shake the Japanese nation to its foundations, and would have far greater repercussions and influence on the course of the war than its authors ever dreamed possible.

The plan was initially conceived in a small way early in January 1942 by Captain Francis Low, an officer on the staff of US Navy C-in-C Admiral Ernest King. He had been to inspect work on the new aircraft carrier USS *Hornet*, commissioned in the previous October and now about to receive the first of her air squadrons at Norfolk, Virginia, and had watched with interest as the navy pilots practised deck landings and take-offs on a 500 ft (150 metre) strip marked out on the airfield adjacent to the shipyard.

Low had been wondering for some time about the possibility of carrying out an air strike on Japan. To use ordinary carrier aircraft would be out of the question; their range was not great enough, and any task force would have to sail almost to within sight of the enemy coast before launching an attack. But suppose, thought Low, that the Army had a bomber with sufficient range, and the ability to take off in 500 ft (150 metres) with a load of fuel and bombs on board – then why not put a few of them on a carrier like the *Hornet* and hit targets on the Japanese mainland, recovering afterwards to bases in friendly territory?

He put the idea to Admiral King, who instructed him to discuss it with the air officer on his staff, Captain Donald Duncan, and present a full report on its feasibility. Duncan was enthusiastic, and immediately started to work out some figures. An experienced pilot, he quickly realized that only one aircraft type might be suitable: the North American B-25 Mitchell medium bomber. Powered by two 1,700 hp Wright Cyclone engines, the first B-25 had flown in August 1940, the design having been ordered straight off the drawing board in September 1939. The latest version, the B-25B, was well armed with machine-guns in dorsal, ventral and tail turrets, and could carry up to 3,000 lb (1,400 kg) of bombs over a range of 1,300 miles (2,100 km). Its top speed was 300 mph (500 kph) at 15,000 ft (4,500 metres), and it carried a crew of five. However, the B-25B needed at least 1,250 ft (380 metres) of runway to take off safely with a 2,000 lb (900 kg) bomb load; whether it could be made light enough to take off in only 500 ft (150 metres) remained to be seen.

Inside a week, Duncan's feasibility study, fifty pages long, was on Admiral King's desk. King read it through and at once telephoned General H.H. Arnold, the Army Air Force C-in-C, to arrange a meeting. 'Hap' Arnold had become one of the first American military pilots back in 1911 and had always fought hard, sometimes at the risk of his career, to make the United States a strong air power. He was greatly impressed by the scheme, and agreed to send three B-25s to Norfolk so that their take-off characteristics could be tested under various load configurations.

During the next few days, it was found to everyone's amazement that a stripped-down lightly loaded B-25 could actually take off well within the 500 ft (150 metres) that represented a carrier's deck length. Captain Duncan had already recommended that the USS *Hornet*, commanded by the able and talented Captain Marc Mitscher, should be the carrier used in the operation, and one day late in January she put to sea with a single B-25 on board. Thirty miles (50 km) offshore, with the carrier steaming into wind, the B-25 pilot took his bomber roaring down the flight deck, lifted her into the air with 150 ft (45 metres) to spare, and flew back to Norfolk.

Meanwhile, General Arnold had been giving a great deal of thought to the man he would select to organize and lead the operation. He needed someone with tremendous organizational ability; a man who was a highly experienced pilot; and one, moreover, who had the engineering expertise necessary to supervise the technical modifications that would have to be made to the B-25s.

One man, among all the potential candidates, met every requirement admirably. He was Lieutenant-Colonel James H. Doolittle, one of the leading pioneers of American aviation. He had learned to fly with the US Army in 1918, and in the years after the First World War his flying career had been marked by a number of

Jimmy Doolittle, pictured after the war as a Lieutenant-General. (USAF)

notable 'firsts'. He had become the first man to span the American continent with a flight from Florida to California; the first American to pilot an aircraft solely by instruments from take-off to landing; the first American to fly an outside loop; and in 1925 he had won the coveted Schneider Trophy for the United States. He had also been a test pilot for the Army Air Corps, had demonstrated American fighter designs overseas, and – of vital importance to his new assignment – he had obtained the degree of a Doctor of Science in aeronautical engineering at the Massachusetts Institute of Technology.

Jimmy Doolittle had recently retired from Shell – in whose service, incidentally, he had played a leading part in persuading the Army Air Corps to use 100-octane fuel, which greatly increased aero-engine performance – when he was recalled to military service in 1940. He was forty-five years old, at the peak of his aviation career (he had been named president of the Institute of Aeronautical Science some months earlier), and yet he welcomed the chance to get back into uniform. During those months of 1940 and 1941, he sensed that America would soon be in the war, and he wanted to play his part.

During 1941 General Arnold, who was an old friend, used him as a kind of trouble-shooter to deal with the hundreds of problems that arose as the US aircraft industry strove to gear up its resources to meet the growing demand for modern aircraft by the armed forces. This was still his job when Arnold summoned him to Washington and gave him the first details of the daring scheme to bomb Japan.

Like Captain Duncan, Doolittle realized at once that the B-25 was the only suitable aircraft. The problem was to strip it down so that it could take off from the carrier with a sizeable load of fuel and bombs, while not impairing its performance in any way. He made a lot of calculations, which he submitted to Arnold, and the C-in-C told him to get on with the job of modifiying the bombers and training their crews while Duncan set up the whole operation and arranged full co-operation between Navy and Air Force, not the easiest of tasks at the best of times.

While Duncan set off for Pearl Harbor to brief Admiral Chester Nimitz, C-in-C United States Pacific Fleet, who would be responsible for putting a task force together, Doolittle assembled a team of engineers and took a B-25 apart. He removed the ventral gun turret and installed a rubber 60 gal (270 litre) fuel tank in its place, and another rubber tank holding 160 gal (725 litres) was fitted into the catwalk above the bomb bay. Together with the existing fuel tanks, that made a total of 1,050 gal (4,775 litres). He also removed the top-secret Norden bombsight and replaced it with much cheaper and more rudimentary equipment; the attack was going to be made from low level, and Doolittle reckoned that the sophistication of the Norden would not be necessary. Quite apart from that, no one wanted the new sight to fall into enemy hands. New propellers and de-icing equipment were also fitted, while every weighty item – including radios – that was not considered absolutely vital was removed.

After ten days of modifications and trials, Doolittle found himself able to lift a stripped-down B-25 from a 400 ft (120 metre) length of runway while carrying 2,000 lb (900 kg) of bombs and a full fuel load. While modifications to more B-25s went ahead, General Arnold authorized Doolittle to select his crews, and advised him to draw them from the Air Force's most experienced B-25 units, the 17th Bomb Group and the 89th Reconnaissance Squadron, both then based at Lexington County Airport, South Carolina.

Doolittle flew to Lexington early in February and selected twenty-four crews, all of them volunteers. A week later they reported to Eglin Field, near Pensacola in Florida, where they began intensive training with the modified B-25s. They still had not been told the nature of the target, but by this time some of them were making intelligent guesses. Time and again, Doolittle stressed the need for secrecy; the success of their mission, and their lives, depended on it.

While training continued, the naval task force was taking shape. It was to consist of the carriers *Hornet* and *Enterprise*, two heavy cruisers, two light cruisers, eight destroyers and two tankers, and it was to be commanded by Vice-Admiral W.F. 'Bull' Halsey. The latter flew to San Francisco, where he met Doolittle and went over the details of the plan. He was able to clear up one thing that had been bothering Doolittle: whether they would have to push their aircraft unceremoniously over the side if they were attacked, leaving room for *Hornet*'s air squadrons to come on deck and go into action, or whether they would have time to fly off. Halsey told him that they would probably be able to take off and fly to Midway Island if the attack came outside Japanese waters; after that, with Midway out of range, they could either shove their B-25s overboard or take off for Japan, with the prospect of ditching in the China Sea after the raid. If all went well, the *Hornet* would take them as close as possible – but not within 400 miles (650 km) – of the Japanese coast, giving them a sufficient fuel margin to reach China after the attack.

By the middle of March 1942, Doolittle's crews had completed their training, achieving astonishing standards of skill. One pilot even succeeded in taking off after a run of only 287 ft (87.5 metres). They now flew down to McClelland Field near Sacramento, California, where the final maintenance checks were to be made. Afterwards, they took their bombers to Alameda Naval Air Station, near San Francisco, where they finally rendezvoused with their carrier.

Doolittle had decided to take sixteen B-25s on the *Hornet*, and getting them on board was a complex business. Carrier air groups normally fly on when their ships are at sea, but there could be no question of this with the B-25s. They had to be lifted aboard with cranes, and then lashed to the flight deck. They did not have folding wings, like naval aircraft, which ruled out any possibility of their being stowed in the big hangar below decks. When the bombers were all on board the *Hornet* had a distinctly stern-heavy appearance, as though a cluster of huge parasites had suddenly descended on that part of her.

The *Hornet* sailed from Alameda on 2 April. Not until she had been at sea for twenty-four hours did Doolittle brief the crews who had been selected to fly the mission; until now not even his second in command, Major Jack Hilger of the 98th Reconnaissance Squadron, had known the specific nature of the target – or rather targets, for the B-25s were to hit Yokohama, Osaka, Kobe and

Nagoya as well as Tokyo. Every day, during the remainder of the voyage, the pilots spent long hours poring over the bulky target intelligence folders which Doolittle, Low and Duncan had assembled. Before long the layout of their objectives, together with the nature of the terrain they would have to fly over to reach them, was as familiar as the cockpits of their bombers.

The *Hornet* made rendezvous with the other warships of Task Force 16 north of the Hawaiian Islands, and sailed straight on across the Pacific towards the launching point. At dawn on 18 April, the day fixed for the strike, the vessels were still 700 miles (1,100 km) off the Japanese coast, and the weather was worsening, with a high sea running and the wind strength increasing all the time. Adding to all the other worries, a small Japanese ship was sighted at 06.30, and although the cruiser *Northampton* was quickly sent to blow her out of the water, it was certain that if she carried radio she would have had ample time to signal the task force's presence.

Doolittle's original plan had been to take off some time ahead of the others and drop four clusters of incendiary bombs on Tokyo just before nightfall, starting a blaze that would lead the following B-25s straight to the target. Now, because of that one encounter with the Japanese steamer, everything had to be changed. With the possibility that Japanese bombers were even now preparing to take off and attack the task force, Admiral Halsey could not afford to endanger his ships by holding course until they reached the planned launch point, 300 miles (500 km) further on. The take-off would have to be brought forward several hours, and the crews knew what that meant. Even with their overload tanks, the bombers might not have enough fuel to reach China.

Then Jimmy Doolittle hit on a scheme that would help alleviate the fuel problem. He ordered ten 5-gal (23 litre) drums of petrol to be loaded on each aircraft, and told the crew chiefs to use them to top up the ventral fuel tank as its level dropped during the flight. Immediately afterwards, Doolittle summoned all the pilots to a last-minute briefing, in which he emphasized take-off procedure. The *Hornet* was battling her way into the teeth of a 35 mph (55 kph) gale and she was pitching violently, so it was vital that the pilots started their take-off run at exactly the right moment, otherwise they would find themselves taking off uphill or diving into the sea.

The crews filed out to their aircraft and climbed aboard. All eyes were on Doolittle's B-25 as the pilot opened the throttle slowly, holding the bomber against the brakes. The bow of the carrier

North American B-25 Mitchell bombers ranged on the flight deck of the USS Hornet *prior to the Tokyo raid.* (US Navy)

dipped sharply, then began to rise, and at that moment Doolittle released his brakes and gave the engines full power. The B-25 began to move, slowly at first, then gathering speed. With 100 ft (30 metres) to spare Doolittle lifted her cleanly away from the deck and took her up in steep climb, turning and bringing her round in a tight circle, flying over the length of the carrier before setting course. There was a reason for this; the bombers' compasses had been affected by the metal mass of the carrier, so by flying over her while Captain Mitscher held her on a westerly heading the pilots could check the accuracy of their instruments.

All sixteen B-25s took off safely, despite the heaving motion of the carrier, and followed Doolittle's bomber in the direction of Japan. The second B-25 to take off, flown by Lieutenant Travis Hoover, formed up with Doolittle and the two machines flew on together. They had 670 miles (1,070 km) to go to Tokyo, and for the next four and a half hours there was little to do but hold a steady course, flying at the slowest possible economical cruising speed in order to conserve fuel. Doolittle took turns at sharing the controls with his co-pilot, Lieutenant Richard Cole. The other members of his crew were the navigator, Lieutenant Henry Potter, the bombardier, Sergeant Fred Braemer, and the crew chief, Sergeant Paul J. Leonard, who also doubled up as gunner.

They stayed low, as low as 200 ft (60 metres) above the sea. Although the Japanese air defences were not thought to have the benefit of radar, the lower the bombers remained the less the risk of detection by surface vessels or patrol aircraft.

At 13.30, Jimmy Doolittle sighted the enemy coast. Potter told him that they would make landfall 30 miles (48 km) north of Tokyo, and he turned out to be dead right. As they crossed the coast, Doolittle picked out a large lake over on the left, and a quick check with the map confirmed the navigator's accuracy. He turned south, skimming low over a patchwork of fields. Peasants looked up and waved, mistaking the speeding B-25 for one of their own aircraft. Once, Doolittle looked up and saw five Japanese fighters cruising a couple of thousand feet above, but they made no move to attack and eventually turned away. Another good point about this low-level work was that the B-25's drab camouflage blended in nicely with the background, making the bombers extremely difficult to spot from aircraft flying at a higher altitude.

The bombers thundered on, skirting the slopes of hills, leap-frogging high-tension cables. There was no flak; it was just like one of the many training flights back home. Suddenly, dead ahead, was the great sprawling complex of the Japanese capital city, and Doolittle took the B-25 up to 1,500 ft (450 metres). In the glazed nose, bombardier Fred Braemer peered ahead, searching for the munitions factory that was their target. He found it and steered Doolittle towards it, the pilot holding the aircraft rock-steady in response to the bombardier's instructions. On Doolittle's instrument panel a red light blinked four times, each blink denoting the release of an incendiary cluster. The B-25 jumped, lightened of its 2,000 lb (900 kg) load, and Doolittle opened the throttles, anxious to get clear of the target area.

The flight across Tokyo lasted five minutes. Not until they were over the outer suburbs did flak burst across the sky, far in their wake. There was no time to observe the results of their attack: it was full throttle all the way to the coast, their ground speed aided by a 25 mph (45 kph) tail wind.

Behind Doolittle, the fifteen other B-25s were attacking their assigned targets. Travis Hoover released his bombs and fled, following much the same route as Doolittle, while at Yokosuka Lieutenant Edgar E. McElroy, who had been the thirteenth pilot to take off, had an extraordinary stroke of luck. His target was the docks area, and right in the middle of it was the aircraft carrier *Ryuho*. McElroy dropped a 500 lb (225 kg) bomb slap on the flight deck, causing damage that delayed work on the carrier by several weeks. In fact, she took no part in active operations, being surrendered inoperative at Kure at the end of the war. McElroy and his crew got safely away.

Other crews were not so lucky. Lieutenant William G. Farrow hit oil storage tanks and an aircraft factory in the Osaka-Kobe area, got away unscathed, flew to China and baled out with the rest of his crew in bad weather, only to be captutred by pro-Japanese Chinese and turned over to the enemy. He and another crew member, Corporal C. Spatz, were murdered by the Japanese; the other three spent the rest of the war in prison camps.

The B-25 flown by Lieutenant Dean Hallmark also reached China and the crew baled out over Poyang Lake. Two crew members, Sergeant William Dieter and Corporal Donald Fitzmorris, landed in the lake and were drowned; Dean Hallmark was captured and murdered; his co-pilot, Lieutenant Robert Meder, died of starvation in prison camp. The sole survivor of Hallmark's crew was the navigator, Lieutenant Chase Neilson, who spent forty months as a prisoner of war.

Some crews had lucky escapes. Lieutenant Richard O. Joyce, the pilot of the sixteenth B-25, was attacked by nine Zero fighters over Tokyo. Their fire ripped a great gash in the bomber's rear fuselage and fragments peppered the tail, but despite this Joyce succeeded in getting away and baled out with his men over friendly Chinese territory. Another pilot, Ross Greening, was also attacked by fighters; his gunner, Sergeant Melville Gardner, shot down one of them and Greening got away. He and his crew also baled out over China, suffering only minor injuries on landing.

The plan was for all the B-25s to head south-west across the China Sea, skirting the Japanese islands of Shikoku and Kyushu, and fly to the Chinese airfield of Chuchow in Chekiang province. The plan, however, was badly disrupted by the weather. First of all, as Jimmy Doolittle found during the sea crossing, the wind veered, reducing the bombers' ground speed and using up more precious fuel; and then, when they crossed the Chinese coast, they found a thick blanket of cloud stretching as far as the eye could see. Doolittle had been promised that a homing beacon would have been set up at Chuchow, but they could detect no welcoming radio signal from it. In fact, the aircraft carrying it to the field had crashed in the mountains, and it later transpired that the message alerting the Chinese to expect the American bombers had somehow gone astray, so that no one knew they were coming.

Not daring to risk a descent through the murk – there were moutains all around Chuchow, and by this time it was dark – Doolittle ordered his crew to bale out. They were picked up by Chinese troops and eventually arrived at Chuchow to find five crews already there: Major Jack Hilger and Lieutenants Ross Greening, David Jones, William Bower and Robert Gray. Baling out like Doolittle, they had sustained only one casualty: Gray's gunner, Corporal Leland D. Faktor, who had been killed when he fractured his skull on landing.

Considering that Chuchow was surrounded on three sides by Japanese forces, it was incredible that only two crews, Farrow's and Hallmark's, had actually had the misfortune to land in enemy territory. In the twenty-four hours after the raid, reports began to trickle in about the fate of the others. Captain David Jones, Lieutenant Everett Holstrom and their crews were all safe; Lieutenant Ted Lawson had ditched off the coast despite a badly injured leg and he and his men had struggled ashore, where they were sheltered by Chinese guerrillas. Lawson, however, lost his leg. Lieutenant Harold F. Watson and his crew had baled out about 100 miles (160 km) south of Poyand Lake; Watson had suffered a broken arm, but no one else was injured. Lieutenant Donald Smith had landed not far from Lawson, and it was one of his crew, Lieutenant T.R. White, the only medical officer on the flight – who had amputated the injured pilot's leg under appallingly primitive conditions.

That left only Captain Edward J. York unaccounted for, and it was some time before Doolittle learned what had become of him. After bombing Tokyo and heading out to sea, York had discovered that his B-25 had used up far more fuel than should have been the case, and there was no possibility of reaching China. He had therefore turned north and landed on Russian territory 40 miles (65 km) north of Vladivostok. He and his crew were interned, as no state of war existed between the Soviet Union and Japan, and it was only after more than a year of protracted negotiations that the Russians released them.

Of the eighty men who took part in the raid, ten died and fifteen more were injured, in most cases only slightly. Sadly, twelve of Doolittle's gallant band were to die later in the war. Doolittle himself was promoted to the rank of Brigadier-General immediately after the raid and awarded the Medal of Honor. All the other survivors received the Distinguished Flying Cross. Doolittle later commanded the United States Twelfth Army Air Force (AAF) in North Africa, the Fifteenth AAF in Italy and the Eighth AAF in England. In 1946 he rejoined Shell Oil as vice-president, and in 1956 he became Chairman of the National Advisory Committee for Aeronautics. He died in California on 27 September, 1993, and is buried in Arlington National Cemetery beside his wife, Josephine Daniels Doolittle, who predeceased him by five years.

Although most of the targets assigned to the B-25 crews were hit, the damage caused was slight, mainly because the aircraft carried relatively light bomb loads. The effect on the morale of the Japanese, however, flushed by their recent victories, was incalculable. There was also another consequence, and it was to turn the tide of the war in the Pacific.

As a direct result of the Tokyo raid and its impact, Admiral Yamamoto launched an ambitious plan to extend the eastern perimeter of the Japanese defences and bring the American Pacific Fleet, now based on carrier task groups, to battle. The outcome, in June 1942, was the Battle of Midway, when Yamamoto's carrier forces were effectively shattered. Midway marked the beginning of the end for Japan's dreams of conquest, and set the stage for the long Allied push back across the Pacific. Before that push ended, Japan's cities would know an agony of fire and destruction that their inhabitants would never have dreamed possible at the time when Jimmy Doolittle and his men hit the Japanese mainland for the first time.

CHAPTER NINE

Dead on Time

It may be said that the tide of the Pacific war began to turn in the Allies' favour as early as May 1942, when a large Japanese troop convoy, supported by a strong carrier task force, sailed for Port Moresby in eastern New Guinea. The plan was to capture Port Moresby and use it as a springboard for the envelopment of northern and eastern Australia, but it never materialized. On 4 May, the Japanese were met in the Coral Sea by an American task force of roughly equal strength. The opposing fleets never came within sight or gunshot range of each other; the action was fought entirely by naval aircraft. It ended with one aircraft carrier sunk and one damaged on the American side and two damaged on the Japanese side; but despite the latter's technical victory, the troop convoy turned back and the seaborne invasion of Port Moresby was abandoned.

Despite this setback, plans went ahead for a strong Japanese thrust in the central Pacific, with the two-fold aim of capturing Midway Island and destroying what was left of the US Pacific Fleet. The architect of the plan was Admiral Isoroku Yamamoto, C-in-C of the Imperial Japanese Navy's Combined Fleet, and the mastermind behind the attack on Pearl Harbor six months earlier.

Yamamoto was born in 1884. He was an adopted child, his original family name being Takano. He graduated from the Japanese Naval Academy in 1904, and in the following year he saw action in the naval battle at Tsushima during the Russo-Japanese war, losing two fingers. He attended the Naval War College and then went to the United States to study at Harvard. Later, as a captain, he served as Naval Attaché to the United States from 1925 to 1927; he therefore knew the Americans well, and was fluent in English. After serving in a number of posts, he was appointed C-in-C of the Combined Fleet in 1939. In 1940, he made a thorough study of the attack on Taranto naval base by British carrier aircraft,

Admiral Isoroku Yamamoto, one of the most talented naval commanders of modern times. (Author's collection)

which resulted in the crippling of major components of the Italian fleet, and used the lesson to good advantage in planning the much larger attack on Pearl Harbor a year later.

Yamamoto was responsible for planning most Japanese naval operations during this period; but the one he was about to launch against Midway was doomed to go disastrously wrong.

The Japanese thrust was led by a four-carrier mobile force comprising the *Akagi,* the *Kaga,* the *Hiryu* and the *Soryu,* supported by heavy units of the main body (First Fleet) and covered by a diversionary attack by carrier aircraft on Dutch Harbor in the Aleutians. The thrust towards Midway was met by a greatly outnumbered US carrier force composed of Task Force 17 (Rear Admiral F.J. Fletcher) with the USS *Yorktown* and Task Force 16 (Rear Admiral R.A. Spruance) with the USS *Hornet* and the USS

Enterprise, and also by navy, marine and army air units based on Midway.

The opening action of the battle took place on 3 June 1942, when the Japanese fleet was sighted by a Consolidated PBY flying boat. Six Grumman TBF Avengers belonging to a shore-based detachment of Torpedo Squadron 8 (VT-8) were launched to attack the Japanese, together with army B-17s and Marine SB2U Vindicators. None of the Avengers scored a hit and only one returned to Midway. At 07.00 on 4 June the US carriers *Enterprise* and *Hornet* launched their strike groups, fourteen TBDs (Douglas Devastators) of VT-6 and fifteen of TB-8, with Grumman F4Fs of VF-6 flying top cover. VT-8 attacked first and all fifteen aircraft were shot down by Zeros; only one crew member survived. VT-6, attacking the *Kaga,* lost ten aircraft before they reached their dropping points. The *Enterprise*'s air group, attacking the *Soryu* with twelve TBDs of VT-3 and seventeen SBDs (Douglas Dauntlesses) of VB-3, fared no better. Only five TBDs survived to make their torpedo attacks, and three of these were shot down on the way out. Of the forty-one TBDs launched, only six returned to the task force, and one of these ran out of fuel and ditched.

The sacrifice of the three torpedo bomber squadrons was not in vain; they had absorbed the bulk of the Japanese fighter attacks, and the Zeros were still scattered when thirty-seven Dauntless dive-bombers from the *Enterprise*'s VB-5 and the seventeen from *Yorktown*'s VB-3 made their attack, sinking the *Akagi, Kaga* and *Soryu.* The cost to the dive-bombers was sixteen aircraft from the Enterprise air group. A Japanese counter-attack from the *Hiryu* damaged the *Yorktown,* but she returned to full operation after a short time. Then

The Mitsubishi A6M Zero was one of the world's best fighters at the start of the Pacific War, but suffered from a lack of armour protection. (Author's collection)

a second attack was made by six Japanese torpedo bombers; two were shot down, but the other four launched their torpedoes and two hit the carrier, which had to be abandoned. She was later sunk by a submarine. At 17.00, the *Hiryu* was crippled in an attack by twenty-four SBDs from the *Enterprise*; her burned-out hulk was sunk by a Japanese destroyer the next day. At a cost of ninety-two aircraft and the *Yorktown*, the US Navy had destroyed four fleet carriers, three-quarters of the Japanese Navy's carrier striking force.

With control of the air irretrievably lost, the Japanese withdrew under attack by Midway-based and carrier aircraft. Other US losses in the Midway battle included forty shore-based aircraft. In addition to the four carriers, the Japanese lost 258 aircraft and a large percentage of their most experienced carrier pilots, even though many were saved by escorting destroyers. It was a decisive defeat that effectively turned the tide of the Pacific war. A Japanese history of the battle comments:

Special note should be taken of the activities of the Hiryu fighter squadron during the Battle of Midway. Nine carrier fighters under the command of Lt Shigematsu joined the first wave attack; they shot down a total of 18 F4Fs and Buffaloes that rose to intercept them. The unit itself returned safely to the carrier. The three aircraft carriers Akagi, Kaga, and Soryu, however, received hits from attacking American carrier aircraft and were destroyed by fire. The remaining carrier, the Hiryu, was able to send out two waves of attack forces by herself; this force severely damaged the carrier Yorktown. At the same time, casualties on the part of the Hiryu's carrier aircraft were not minor, either. Six carrier fighters served as escort for the Kobayashi carrier bombing squadron, with the exception of two aircraft of the Minegishi Shotai that had to return prematurely to the carrier. The remaining four aircraft shot down seven enemy aircraft during an aerial encounter over the American task force. Our side suffered the loss of three aircraft also; Lt Shigematsu was the sole survivor who returned to the carrier. Four carrier fighters led by Lt Mori and reinforced by two carrier fighters from the Kaga escorted the Tomonaga torpedo attack squadron and participated in the attack on the American task force. After battling in the air with about 30 American fighters, the unit was able to shoot down 11 of the enemy; however, two aircraft, including the one piloted by Lt Mori, were destroyed. On the other hand, to provide combat air patrol directly over the carrier itself, a total of 33 aircraft were used, including planes that had been sent to the Hiryu from other carriers. By evening and the tenth watch, a cumulative total of 33 enemy aircraft had been shot down. At the same time, five Hiryu-based fighters among others were also lost. As a matter of fact, the entire fighter squadron (aircraft) complement was wiped out. Also, the carrier Hiryu *itself received bomb hits during the afternoon raids conducted on her, caught on fire, and sank the next morning. The Battle of Midway ended as a crushing defeat for the Japanese.*

For America, the long fight back across the Pacific began on 7 August 1942, when a division of United States marines stormed ashore on Guadalcanal in the Solomon Islands. It was an event that was to play a key part in the downfall, eight months later, of Admiral Yamamoto.

One of the primary objectives was an airfield the Japanese had built. The marines moved in and took it, and the land battle subsequently centred on this vital jungle airstrip, renamed Henderson Field by the Americans in honour of Major Lofton P. Henderson, who had lost his life leading US Marine Corps dive-bombers into action against the Japanese from Midway. The marines hung on desperately in one of the most heroic and tenacious actions of the Pacific war, and by 20 August the strip had been made secure enough for the first American fighters and bombers to fly in from the carrier force which had been providing air support for the marines until then. Land-based air support initially comprised the Grumman F4F Wildcats of Marine Fighter Squadrons VMF-223 and VMF-224 and the Douglas SBD Dauntless dive-bombers of VMSB-231 and VMSB-232.

On 23 August, land-based bombers from Henderson Field and strike aircraft from the USS *Saratoga* set out in search of Japanese surface units located by US scouting seaplanes, but failed to find the enemy in bad weather. On the 24th, during what became known as the Battle of the Eastern Solomons, strike aircraft from the light carrier *Ryujo* were intercepted by Grumman Wildcats from Guadalcanal and heavily defeated; the *Ryujo* herself was sunk in an attack by thirty SBD dive-bombers and eight Avengers. Some of her aircraft managed to land on Rabaul, but all her fighters were lost when they had to ditch; most of the pilots were picked up.

The climax of a Japanese plan to neutralize and capture Guadalcanal's vital airstrip, as a preliminary to the destruction of the remaining US air resources in the Solomons, was an action known as the battle of Santa Cruz, on 26–27 October 1942. At this point the US Navy had only two carriers in the area, the USS *Enterprise* and the USS *Hornet*, the latter having replaced the USS *Saratoga*, damaged by a submarine torpedo on 31 August and withdrawn to Pearl Harbor for repair. The Americans had also lost the carrier USS *Wasp*, sunk by a submarine on 15 September while escorting a troop convoy to Guadalcanal. To activate their plan, the Japanese naval forces put to sea from Truk on 11 October. They included: the Carrier Striking Force with the *Shokaku* and *Zuikaku*, the light carrier *Zuiho* and seven destroyers; the Advance Striking Force with two new carriers, the *Junyo* and *Hiyo,* supported by two battleships, five cruisers and thirteen destroyers; and the Battleship Striking Force, with two battleships, three cruisers and eight destroyers. On 26 October the opposing carrier task forces made contact almost simultaneously and launched their strike aircraft. The Japanese force, in two waves forty-five minutes apart, comprised forty-two Aichi D3A2 dive-bombers, thirty-six Mitsubishi B5N2 Kate torpedo-bombers, and fifty-five Zero fighters from the *Shokaku,* the *Zuikaku* and the *Zuiho;* the *Hornet* and the *Enterprise* launched three waves comprising twenty SBD Dauntlesses, twenty TBM Avengers and twenty-four F4F Wildcats. While these forces were *en route*, two SBDs from the *Enterprise*, on an armed reconnaissance, encountered the *Zuiho* and bombed her, damaging her flight deck and rendering it unusable.

At 09.40, purely by chance, the opposing air groups ran into each other and a brief air battle developed in which the Zeros shot down three SBDs and four Wildcats for the loss of five of their own. At 10.10, the first Japanese wave located the *Hornet* and subjected her to a bomb and torpedo attack that left her burning and listing in the water. Thirty minutes later, the *Hornet*'s strike aircraft also found the *Shokaku* and scored four hits with 1,000 lb (450 kg) bombs, putting the carrier out of the battle. She limped back to Japan to undergo repairs, a process that would last until the end of February 1943. The Japanese second wave attacked the *Enterprise*, scoring three bomb hits; torpedo attacks were frustrated by Wildcat combat air patrols. Further attacks in the afternoon, launched by the *Zuikaku* and the *Junyo*, succeeded in sinking the crippled *Hornet*. Fortunately for the Americans, the Japanese were unable to exploit their tactical success. They had exhausted their fuel reserves and were compelled to withdraw to Truk to replenish.

The air fighting in the Solomons clearly showed that the Zero, while still superior to the American types it encountered, no longer enjoyed the complete mastery of the air that had been the hallmark of its operations in the early months of the Pacific war. During this period it was the Grumman F4F Wildcat that held the line, and as the US Navy and Marine Corps pilots gained more combat

Marines extinguish an engine fire in a Grumman F4F Wildcat on Guadalcanal in 1942. For a year, the Wildcat held the line against much superior enemy fighters like the Zero. (Author's collection)

experience and developed better tactics, they began to take an increasing toll of the enemy. And, in terms of equipment, much better prospects were just over the horizon.

One of the new combat aircraft to make its appearance in the Pacific theatre early in late 1942 was the Lockheed P-38 Lightning. Although it tended to be overshadowed by the Republic P-47 Thunderbolt and the North American P-51 Mustang, the P-38 was a very effective long-range tactical fighter and was to play a vital part in winning air superiority for the Allies, particularly in the Pacific theatre. Distinctive with its twin tail booms, the P-38 was designed to meet the exacting requirements of a 1937 US Army Air Corps specification, calling for a high-altitude interceptor capable

The prototype Lockheed XP-38. An unconventional and innovative design, the P-38 had a very useful combat radius. (Lockheed)

of 360 mph (575 kph) at 20,000 ft (6,000 metres) and 290 mph (465 kph) at sea level. The sole XP-38 prototype flew on 27 January 1939 and was followed by thirteen YP-38 evaluation aircraft with more powerful V-1710 engines and a nose armament of four machine-guns and a 37 mm cannon. An initial production batch of thirty P-38s was built, these being delivered from the summer of 1941; the next production model was the P-38D, thirty-six of which were produced. In November 1941 the P-38E appeared, with a more powerful armament. The P-38F, which appeared early in 1942, was the first variant to be used in large numbers, operating in Europe from the summer of 1942 and in North Africa from November; 527 were built. This was followed by the P-38G (1082) and P-38H (601), these variants featuring either armament or engine changes.

The first Lightnings actually arrived in the Pacific in April 1942, but these were four examples of the F-4 reconnaissance variant, deployed to Australia with the 8th Photographic Reconnaissance Squadron. The first fighter Lightnings to arrive in Australia comprised twenty-five P-38Fs assigned to the 39th Fighter Squadron of the 35th Fighter Group, which moved up to Jackson Field, Port Moresby, and went into action in November 1942. The squadron achieved its first combat success on 27 December, when it destroyed eleven Japanese aircraft for the loss of one P-38. The second Fifth Air Force unit to receive Lightnings was the 8th Fighter Group, with the 49th equipping shortly afterwards.

The Thirteenth Air Force, operating out of the Solomons, also wanted the fast, heavily armed Lightning because of its range and twin-engined capability, both enormous advantages when operating over the vast expanses of the south-west Pacific. On 3 October 1942 the 347th Fighter Group was activated in New Caledonia, one of its squadrons, the 339th, being equipped with P-38s.

The CO of the 339th Fighter Squadron was 27-year-old Major John Mitchell, a Mississippian who had arrived in the Pacific theatre in January 1942 with one of the 347th FG's other squadrons, the 70th, which flew Bell P-39 Airacobras. In October 1942, after several months of training in Fiji, Mitchell and eight other pilots were sent to Guadalcanal for combat duty with the 339th FS, which at that time also operated the P-39. In November, Mitchell assumed command of the 339th, which had now begun to receive its first P-38s.

Meanwhile, the planners of Japan's Imperial General Command were preoccupied with retaining their strategic base on Rabaul, and to this end they spared no effort to strengthen their bases in the Solomons and New Guinea. If they could not hold the outposts to Fortress Rabaul, at least they could make every Allied advance a costly and time-consuming task. While they did what they could to disrupt Allied preparations, they sought to improve their position in the threatened area. When these efforts failed, they assembled all their resources for an ambitious and desperate attempt to smash Allied air power and cut the enemy's line of communications. The onus of this operation, devised by Admiral Yamamoto's staff and named 'I-Go', fell on the 11th Air Fleet, whose assets were strengthened by aircraft stripped from bases on Truk and from the Japanese aircraft carriers.

On 3 April 1943, Admiral Yamamoto flew to Rabaul to supervise the air offensive, which was due to be launched on the 4th to coincide with his birthday. Bad weather, however, kept the aircraft grounded until the 7th, when Yamamoto, resplendent in his white dress uniform, watched the first of 200 fighters and bombers take

off from Rabaul and head south-east for Guadalcanal in the biggest
Japanese air strike since Pearl Harbor. The attacking force
succeeded in sinking the US destroyer *Aaron Ward*, the tanker
Kanawha and the New Zealand corvette *Moa*, but Japanese losses
were high and returning crews brought back greatly exaggerated
tales of the damage inflicted on the Allied naval forces. In fact, they
claimed to have sunk a cruiser and twenty-five transports, and to
have destroyed 200 Allied aircraft.

Yamamoto, perhaps suspecting that the claims were exaggerated
but none the less believing that the air offensive was succeeding,
decided to make a personal tour of the airfields to spur the crews
on to even greater efforts. The appropriate orders were issued, and
signals were sent to the commanders of the bases concerned,
advising them of the C-inC's schedule.

At Dutch Harbour, Alaska, the United States Navy maintained a
listening post, buried deep underground. There, twenty-four hours
a day, naval intelligence personnel monitored Japanese signals
traffic, intercepted by the seven 300 ft (90 metres) radio masts
mounted on the cliffs above. At 06.36 on 14 April, 1943, the station
picked up a coded signal from Truk. As it had the call sign of
Yamamoto's flagship, the *Yamato* – the biggest battleship in the
world – it was relayed to Washington with top priority, via Kiska,
Kodiak, Elmendorf and San Francisco.

In the intelligence centre at Arlington Hall, Virginia, cryptographers
set about deciphering the signal. The Japanese naval code had been
in the possession of US Intelligence since the late 1930s, and its secrets
were now used to good effect. The enemy signal, from C-in-C South-
eastern Air Fleet to an addressee believed to be the garrison
commander at Bellele, on Bougainville, was almost completely
deciphered by 11.00. It read:

> On 18 April C-in-C Combined Fleet will visit RYZ, R – and RXP
> in accordance with the following schedule:
> 1. Depart RR at 06.00 in a medium attack plane escorted by 6
> fighters arrive RXZ at 08.00. Proceed by minesweeper to R – arriving
> at 08.40.
> 2. At each of the above places the Commander-in-Chief will make a
> tour of inspection and at — he will visit the sick and wounded but
> current operations should continue.

Shortly before noon the translated signal reached the desk of Frank
Knox, Secretary of the Navy. As it apparently referred to a routine

tour of inspection, it did not seem to be of any tactical or strategic interest, and Knox went off to lunch. During the meal, his interest in the signal was awakened by a chance remark made by his private secretary, who quoted the old dictum that wars might be settled by individual duels between commanders.

What if Yamamoto's aircraft could be intercepted by long-range American fighters from Guadalcanal and shot down? The death of the Japanese Naval C-in-C might not win the Pacific war, but it would certainly have a profound effect on future operations.

Knox contacted General H.H. Arnold, Commanding General of the United States Army Air Forces, who in turn approached Colonel Charles Lindbergh, the celebrated aviator who had made the first solo crossing of the Atlantic in 1927 and who was now experimenting with cruise-control techniques aimed at increasing the range of the P-38. Also involved in the discussions was Frank Meyer, of Lockheed's experimental department. After studying the situation, the experts were of the opinion that it should be possible for P-38s from Guadalcanal to intercept Yamamoto, but only if auxiliary fuel tanks could be shipped out to them in time.

The same conclusion had also been reached by Admiral Chester Nimitz, C-in-C of the Pacific Fleet. He signalled Admiral Halsey, commanding the Allied naval forces in the South Pacific, and authorized him to begin preliminary planning for an operation to kill Yamamoto. Nimitz sought, and obtained, the approval of President Roosevelt, who had already been advised of the situation by Frank Knox; the latter, leaving no stone unturned, had also sought the advice of leading churchmen on the morality of killing enemy leaders. No one saw it as much of a problem, and on 15 April Nimitz authorized the mission, code-named Operation Vengeance, to proceed.

At 15.35 on 17 April Navy Secretary Frank Knox personally signed two signals. The first was relayed to General George C. Kenney, commanding the US Fifth Army Air Force, and concerned the provision of auxiliary fuel tanks. This signal was passed on to the Air Force Ordnance Depot at Port Moresby. Three hours later, four B-24 Liberators took off from Milne Bay airstrip carrying eighteen 310 gal (1,400 litre) drop tanks and a similar number of 165 gal (750 litre) drop tanks, bound for Henderson Field.

The second signal, relayed via Pearl Harbor, was destined for the Fighter Control Centre at Henderson Field. Its arrival, at 16.00, coincided with a strong Japanese air attack, which was beaten off by F4U Corsairs of Marine Fighter Squadron VMF-124. It was an

hour before the planners were able to turn their attention to the fine
details of Operation Vengeance.

At 15.10, Major John Mitchell was summoned from the 339th
Squadron's dispersal. A jeep collected him and his two flight
commanders, Lieutenants Thomas G. Lanphier and Beasby Holmes,
and took them to the joint navy and army headquarters at
Tassafaronga, hidden in a palm grove about 9 miles (14 km) from
Henderson. Twenty or so officers were squelching among the puddles
that had formed in the HQ's interior following a recent rainstorm; the
most senior was Rear Admiral Marc A. Mitscher, who had arrived on
Guadalcanal earlier in April to take command of the Allied units there.
Mitchell was handed the signal from Washington. It read:

*Washington, 17.4.43, 15.35. Top Secret, Secretary Navy to Fighter
Control Henderson.*

*Admiral Yamamoto accompanied chief of staff and several general
officers Imperial Navy including surgeon admiral grand fleet left Truk
this morning eight hours for air trip inspection Bougainville bases stop
Admiral and party travelling in two 'Sallys' escorted six Zekes stop
escort of honour from Kahili probable stop Admiral's itinerary colon
arrive Rabaul Bucka 16.30 hours where spend night stop Leave dawn
for Kahili where time of arrival 09.45 hours stop Admiral then to board
submarine chaser for inspection naval units under Admiral Tanaka stop.*

*Squadron 339 P-38 must at all costs reach and destroy Yamamoto
and staff morning April eighteen stop Auxiliary tanks and consumption
data will arrive from Port Moresby evening seventeenth stop
Intelligence stresses extreme punctuality stop President attaches
extreme importance this operation stop Communicate result at once stop
Frank Knox Secretary of State for Navy.*

There was one error in the signal. Yamamoto would not be flying
in a 'Sally' – the Allied code-name for the Mitsubishi Ki21 heavy
bomber – but in a Mitsubishi G4M attack bomber, code-named
'Betty'. Zeke was the Allied code-name for the Mitsubishi A6M
fighter, universally known as the Zero.

It was clear that the success of Operation Vengeance depended
on extremely accurate timing. Admiral Yamamoto was known to
be a stickler for punctuality; if his schedule stated that he was to
arive at Kahili at 09.45, that timing would be accurate to the minute.

That evening, Mitchell pored over maps of the Solomons with
Lanphier and Captain Joe McGuigan, the 339th's intelligence

officer. From Guadalcanal, they plotted a course that would keep them 50 miles (80 km) clear of the Japanese-held islands of New Georgia, Vella Lavella, and the Treasuries. The planned route from Guadalcanal to the interception point at Bougainville covered a distance of 400 miles (650 km), with a flight time of two hours. Based on their estimates of Yamamoto's air speed (180 mph (290 kph)) and scheduled time of arrival at Kahili, they estimated that he would be at the interception point, about 30 miles (50 km) east of Kahili, at 09.35. A plan, suggested by Navy officers, to attack and sink the submarine chaser carrying Yamamoto during the seaborne phase of his journey was dismissed; even if the ship were sunk, there was no guarantee that the admiral would be killed.

At 21.00, the first of the Liberators carrying the auxiliary fuel tanks arrived at Henderson Field in the middle of a fierce thunderstorm, followed by the other three. Ground crews at once began fitting the tanks to the P-38s, working by the light of electric torches in torrential rain and pitch darkness. With great difficulty, the large, cumbersome tanks were installed, two to each aircraft, attached to improvised underwing stations on either side of the central fuselage nacelle, inboard of the engines. Malarial mosquitoes, attracted by the torchlight, plagued the men as they worked.

Shortly before midnight, Mitchell assembled his pilots and briefed them on the mission, which would be flown by the squadron's eighteen most experienced pilots. The aircraft would be split into three groups, a killer group and two covering groups. The pilots assigned to the killer group, charged with the destruction of Yamamoto's aircraft, were Lieutenants Tom Lanphier, Rex Barber, Joe Moore and James MacLanahan. The first cover group of six aircraft would comprise Mitchell, Doug Canning, Jack Jacobson, Beasby Holmes, Ray Hine, and Goerke. Holmes and Hine were to act as reserves for the killer group. The second cover group comprised eight pilots of the 12th Squadron, led by Captain Louis Kittel.

The Lightnings began their take-off at 07.00 on 18 April, and the mission hit trouble almost immediately when Jim MacLanahan's aircraft burst a tyre, skidded, slewed off the end of the runway as its undercarriage folded up, and burst into flames. The pilot got out unharmed. A second casualty was Joe Moore, whose auxiliary tanks refused to feed fuel through the system. After several failed attempts to switch from the main tanks to the auxiliariies, he knew that he had no alternative but to turn back. The remaining sixteen P-38s flew on, maintaining strict radio silence and keeping low over the sea.

By 08.00, the American fighters were 285 miles (455 km) from the planned interception; at that minute, Admiral Yamamoto's 'Betty' bomber took off from Rabaul, precisely on time for his scheduled 10.00 arrival on Bougainville. His entourage included one other 'Betty' bomber and six Zeros of Air Group 204 from Rabaul, led by Sub-Lieutenant Takeshi. One reason for the comparatively light escort was that the Japanese command at Rabaul did not believe that any US aircraft could present a threat at such a range; the Japanese were also unaware that the Americans had deciphered their navy code, so that the exact timing of Yamamoto's flight was known. Yamamoto's chief of staff, Admiral Ugaki, flew in the second bomber.

The sun beat down on the large perspex cockpit glazing of the Lightnings. Designed for high-altitude work, Lockheed had elected not to provide the cockpits with coolers. The pilots sweating profusely, at 08.20 they changed their heading for the first time, swinging slightly to the north. Half an hour later, when abreast of Vella Lavella, they made their second planned course change, again shifting a little more to the north.

Two hours into the flight the pilots were experiencing extreme discomfort because of the sweaty, cramped conditions in their cockpits and the constant strain of flying low over the sea. It came as a massive relief when, at 09.00, Mitchell made their last change, heading north-east towards the coast of Bougainville, 40 miles (65 km) away, and began the slow climb for altitude. Each pilot fired a short burst to test his guns. The minutes ticked away and the Lightnings droned on, climbing as the mountains of Bougainville came into view.

It was Doug Canning who spotted their target, at 09.34, calling out, 'Bogeys, eleven o'clock high.' Mitchell could hardly believe it; there they were, right on schedule, exactly as planned, above and a little to the left. They were flying in formation at about 4,500 ft (1,350 metres). The two 'Betty' bombers were together, the Zero fighter escort about 1,500 ft (450 metres) higher up and a short distance astern, flying in two sections of three. At this point the enemy aircraft were some 3 miles (5 km) distant, heading down the southern coastline of Bougainville towards Kahili.

The Lightning pilots opened up to 3,000 revs, pushed the propeller controls to combat pitch, switched to the main fuel tanks and jettisoned the auxiliaries. John Mitchell, leading the covering force, took his aircraft up in a steady climb at 2,200 ft (670 metres) per minute, eventually reaching 18,000 ft (5,500 metres). Meanwhile, the killer group – now reduced to Lanphier and Barber, as Holmes was having trouble getting rid of his auxiliary tanks and Ray Hine, who had taken MacLanahan's place, was staying with him until he succeeded – closed in on the enemy formation, which was now only 1,000 ft (300 metres) or so above and 2 miles (3 km) distant. The leading G4M 'Betty' was a uniform khaki colour, the second aircraft light grey with a camouflage pattern of green stripes. It was accompanied by six Zeros, three on each side. The P-38 pilots reasoned that this must be Yamamoto's aircraft.

Lanphier and Barber, flying parallel to the enemy, now turned in towards the Japanese formation, aiming to get between it and the island. As they closed in at 280 mph (450 kph) the Japanese pilots saw them at last. The Zeros dropped their belly tanks and the two 'Bettys' began to take evasive action, one going into a 360 degree diving turn and the other heading towards the shoreline.

The US Army Intelligence summary of the operation tells what happened next.

The Zeros dropped their belly tanks and three peeled down, in a string, to intercept Lanphier. When he saw that he could not reach the bomber he turned up and into the Zeros, exploding the first, and firing into the others as they passed. By this time he had reached 6,000 feet [1,800 metres], so he nosed over, and went down to the treetops after his escaping objective. He came into it broadside – fired his bursts – a wing flew off and the plane went flaming to earth.

The Zeros were now pursuing him and had the benefit of altitude. His mission accomplished, he hedgehopped the tree tops and made desperate maneuvers to escape. He kicked rudders, slipped and skidded, tracers were flying past his plane, – but he finally outran them. In all the action he had received two 7.7's in his horizontal stabilizer.

Barber had gone with Lanphier on the initial attack. He went for one of the bombers but its maneuvers caused him to overshoot a little. he whipped back, however, and although pursued by Zeros, caught the bomber and destroyed it. When he fired, the tail section flew off, the bomber turned over on its back and plummetted to earth.

By this time, Holmes had been able to drop his tank and with Hine, who had stayed in formation with him, came in toward the Zeros who were pursuing Barber. A dogfight ensued, many shots were exchanged, but results were not observed. The flight was on its way out of the combat area (in the neighborhood of enemy bases at Kahili, Ballale, and Shortland-Faisi) when Holmes noticed a stray bomber flying low over the water. He dove on it, his bursts getting it smoking in the left engine; Hine also shot at it and Barber polished it off with a burst in the fuselage.

The bomber exploded 'right in my face', a piece of the plane flew off, out through his left wing and knocked out his left inner cooler and other chunks left paint streaks on his wing – so close was his attack driven home.

Holmes, Hine and Barber then turned for home, their mission – to destroy the bombers – a complete success. However, Zeros were coming in on Barber's tail and Holmes whipped up and around and shot one down in flames. Another attempt to draw away ended in another dogfight during which Barber exploded a further Zero. During these minutes, Hine's left engine started to smoke and he was last seen losing altitude south of Shortland Island. It is believed that Hine also accounted for a Zero as a total of three enemy fighters were seen to fall into the sea during this part of the combat.

This report gives the impression that three 'Betty' bombers were shot down, but in fact there were only two in the area. One of them was shot down into the sea by Holmes, some of the crew and passengers – including Admiral Ugaki – surviving, so it seems clear that Lanphier and Barber had attacked the same aircraft. It was a situation that led to much acrimony, as each pilot claimed to have destroyed the 'Betty', but this could not detract from the fact that

Tommy Lanphier, his face in shadow, is decorated at Henderson Field after the mission to kill Yamamoto. (Author's collection)

The remains of Yamamoto's 'Betty' bomber were found again in the jungle many years after the war. (Author's collection)

the mission had been accomplished and that Yamamoto, a victim of his own punctuality, had become quite literally 'dead on time'.

Tommy Lanphier ended the war as a colonel, with seven aerial victories to his credit. He later entered politics and died in San Diego on 26 November, 1987. Rex Barber also finished the war as a colonel, settling in Idaho. He, too, died in 1987. John Mitchell went on to have a distinguished career in the postwar USAF, commanding the 51st Fighter Wing in the later stages of the Korean War, during which he shot down four MiG-15 jet fighters. Retiring as a colonel after twenty-three years of service, he died on 15 November, 1995.

A Japanese patrol hacked its way through the jungle to where the wreckage of Yamamoto's aircraft lay. The admiral was still strapped into his seat, leaning forward over his samurai sword. A single bullet through the head had killed him. His body was cremated on the spot with full ceremony, his ashes and sword being taken back to Tokyo for an impressive military funeral.

Admiral Matome Ugaki recovered from the injuries he had sustained in the crash of the second 'Betty' and was eventually placed in charge of Japan's air defences. On 15 August, 1945, the day of Japan's surrender, Ugaki – whose orders had sent many young Japanese suicide pilots to their deaths – took off himself on what was to be the war's last Kamikaze mission, and was never seen again.

CHAPTER TEN

Battle of the Power Stations

N
o. 487 Squadron, RNZAF, formed part of No. 2 Group, RAF Bomber Command. It was formed at Feltwell, Norfolk, on 15 August 1942 as a light day bomber squadron, equipped with Lockheed Ventura II aircraft. A military development of the civilian Lockheed Model 18 Lodestar, the Ventura was produced to meet a British requirement for an aircraft to replace the Bristol Blenheim in No. 2 Group and the Lockheed Hudson in RAF Coastal Command.

The Lockheed Ventura, seen here in its US B-34 version, had a relatively short career with RAF Bomber Command.

No. 487 had an interesting badge. It depicted a *tekoteko*, a grotesque Maori carved figure that usually adorned the apex of the gable above the entrance to the *whare-whakairo*, the meeting house of a Maori tribe. The *tekoteko* generally brandished a weapon as a challenge to all comers; in this case, the weapon was a bomb. The squadron's motto, in the Maori language, was an appropriate one: *Ki te mutunga – Through to the end.*

The squadron began operations on 6 December 1942, when it contributed sixteen Venturas of the ninety-three aircraft of No. 2 Group – Douglas Bostons, Venturas and de Havilland Mosquitoes – despatched to attack the Philips radio and valve factory at Eindhoven, which was believed to produce about a third of Germany's supply of radio components. The target consisted of two clusters of buildings covering an area of about 70 acres (28 ha), and it was particularly attractive because it was surrounded by open country, a fact that reduced the risk of inflicting civilian casualties on the Dutch down to an absolute minimum.

The attack was made at low level, with the aircraft flying in three waves; the first consisting of thirty-six Bostons, the second of ten Mosquitoes and the third of forty-seven Venturas. However, all did not go according to plan. The bombers were harried by enemy fighters long before they reached the target; the leading formation became dislocated and arrived late over the objective, becoming tangled up with the Mosquitoes in the second wave. Afterwards, instead of re-forming into one compact defensive formation, the bombers straggled back to base in small groups.

The Philips factory had been badly damaged, but the cost to the attacking force had been high. Nine Venturas, five Bostons and a Mosquito failed to return, and another thirty-seven Venturas, thirteen Bostons and three Mosquitoes were damaged. Enemy fighters had accounted for some of the missing aircraft, but the main body of Messerschmitts and Focke-Wulfs had been drawn away from the area by a diversionary attack on Lille carried out by the USAAF. Many of the losses sustained by the Ventura formations, which had attacked at a considerably lower level than the others, had been caused by aircraft colliding with unseen obstacles in the smoke over the target, and some had been shot down by light flak. Of the damaged aircraft that returned to base, thirty-one had suffered bird strikes, a hazard that accompanied all low-level daylight operations. The result did not encourage future operations of this kind, and the unsuitablity of the Ventura as a day bomber

The attack on the Philips factory at Eindhoven, Holland, on 6 December 1943, seen by the camera in one of the attacking aircraft. (Author's collection)

was further underlined by the outcome of an operation on 3 May 1943.

During that month RAF Bomber Command and the US Eighth Army Air Force carried out a series of intensive attacks on power station in Holland, which were supplying energy to the German war effort. All these missions were flown in daylight and the cost in aircraft and crews was high. On 3 May eleven Venturas of No 487 Squadron, Royal New Zealand Air Force, led by Wing Commander Leonard Trent, took off from their base at Methwold in Norfolk to attack the main power station in Amsterdam. Apart from disrupting the power supply to German-controlled industries in the area, the raid was designed to encourage Dutch workers in their resistance to enemy pressure. The importance of bombing the target, which was heavily defended, was strongly impressed on the crews taking part in the operation, and before take-off Trent told his deputy that he intended to go in whatever happened.

Everything went well until the eleven Venturas and their fighter escort were over the Dutch coast, when one of the bombers was hit by flak and had to turn back. A minute later large numbers of enemy fighters appeared; these engaged the Spitfire escort, which soon lost touch with the Venturas. The latter closed up tightly for mutual protection and started their run towards the target, expecting to rendezvous with much more friendly fighters over Amsterdam, but the fighters had arrived in the target area much too soon and had been recalled.

Within moments the Venturas were being savagely attacked by twenty Messerschmitts and Focke-Wulfs. One after the other, six of the bombers went down in flames in the space of four minutes. The remaining four, with Trent at their head, continued doggedly towards the target. The dwindling formation now ran into murderous anti-aircraft fire, which accouted for two more Venturas. Trent and the other surviving crew made accurate bombing runs, harassed all the time by enemy fighters that braved their own flak to press home their attacks. Trent got in a lucky burst with his nose gun at a Focke-Wulf 190, which flicked into a spin and crashed. A moment later the other Ventura received a direct hit and exploded. Trent turned away from the target area, but his aircraft too was hit and began to break up. Trent and his navigator were thrown clear and became prisoners of war; the other two crew members were killed. After the war, when the full story of the raid emerged, Trent was awarded the Victoria Cross.

One of the problems during this period was the relative ineffectiveness of the fighter escort. The RAF fighter squadrons responsible for escorting the bombers of No. 2 Group were equipped with the Spitfire Mk VB, which was outclassed by the Focke-Wulf 190. One of the fighter squadrons was No. 118, which was based at Coltishall, Norfolk, early in 1943. An extract from its war diary, dated 29 January 1943, is revealing.

In the afternoon the Squadron made rendezvous with No. 167 and twelve Venturas over Mundesley and flew at sea level to within a few miles of the Dutch coast, then climbed to 9,000 feet over Ijmuiden. As we crossed the coast four Fw 190s were seen breaking cloud below at 2,000 feet. Our allotted task was to give cover to the bombers which, instead of bombing immediately, went inland for ten minutes then turned round and bombed from east to west on an outward heading. Squadron Leader Wooton decided not to go down for the 190s until the bombers had carried out their task, or while they were still in danger of being attacked. While the bombers and escorts were making their incursion the 190s climbed up and were joined by others, but before they could attack the bombers they were engaged by 118 Squadron. In the resultant dog-fight, of which no-one seemed to have a very clear picture, Sgt Lack destroyed an Fw 190 which he followed down to sea level and set on fire; it was eventually seen to crash into the sea by Hallingworth.

Hallingworth was attacked and his aircraft hit, and he in turn claimed a 190 damaged. The CO, who engaged the leading Fw 190, also claimed one damaged, the enemy aircraft breaking away after being hit by cannon fire and going down followed by Sgt Buglass, who lost sight of it. Shepherd went to Hallingworth's rescue when he was being attacked, and was himself fired at head-on by two Fw 190s. Flight Sergeant Cross is missing from this engagement; no-one saw what happened to him, but as he was flying number two to Shepherd it is believed that he must have been hit during the double attack on his section leader. The Squadron got split up during the engagement, seven aircraft coming back together and the other four in two pairs. No-one saw Cross crash. He was a very nice, quiet Canadian and will be very much missed …

In March 1943 an important new American medium bomber, the Martin B-26 Marauder, arrived in the European theatre of operations. One of the most controversial Allied medium bombers of the Second World War, at least in the early stages of its career, the Glenn L. Martin 179 was entered in a US Army light and medium bomber competition of 1939. Its designer, Peyton M. Magruder, placed the emphasis on high speed, producing an aircraft with a torpedo-like fuselage, two massive radial engines, tricycle undercarriage and stubby wings. The advanced nature of the aircraft's design proved so impressive that an immediate order was placed for 201 examples off the drawing board, without a prototype. The first B-26 flew on 25 November 1940, powered by two Pratt & Whitney R-2800-5 engines; by this time, orders for 1,131 B-26A and B-26B bombers had been received. The first unit to rearm with a mixture of B-26s and B-26As was the 22nd Bombardment Group at Langley Field in February 1941. Early in 1942 it moved to Australia, where it became part of the US Fifth Air Force, attacking enemy shipping, airfields and installations in New Guinea and New Britain. It carried out its first attack, a raid on Rabaul, on 5 April 1942.

The Marauder had a bad reputation, and in its early months of service it had an appalling accident rate. The problem was that it was unusually heavy for a twin-engined machine, and as a consequence it needed extra care in handling, particularly in the take-off and landing configurations. It killed a lot of inexperienced pilots before the Air Corps got used to it, and in its early days it earned a totally unjustified reputation for being a lethal aircraft. In action, however, with experienced crews, the B-26 was superb.

The first Marauders assigned to the European theatre arrived in March 1943, equipping the 322nd Bombardment Group of the 3rd Bombardment Wing at Great Saling, near Braintree in Essex. The group immediately began training for low-level attack missions under the operational control of the US Eighth Army Air Force. Some senior USAAF officers believed that assigning the B-26 to the low-level attack role in Europe was a serious mistake, arguing that the Japanese AA defences in New Guinea were nothing in comparison with the weight of metal the Germans could throw up. The flak and the fighters would tear the B-26s to pieces.

Despite these grim warnings, training continued unchecked and the first low-level mission was scheduled for 14 May 1943. The target was the Velsen power station at Ijmuiden, in Holland, which had twice been unsuccessfully attacked by the RAF. The American raid went ahead as planned; twelve B-26s set out, one aborted with engine trouble, and the remainder attacked the objective through intense flak at heights of between 100 and 300 ft (30–90 metres). One B-26 was destroyed in a crash-landing on returning to base;

the rest all got back safely, although all had suffered battle damage. Nevertheless, the crews were jubilant; they had unloaded their delayed-action bombs squarely on the target, and they were convinced that it had been destroyed.

When reconnaissance photographs were developed the next day, however, the Americans were astonished. No damage at all had been inflicted on the power station. It appeared that the enemy had rushed special bomb disposal squads into the area to disarm the bombs, which had been fitted with thirty-minute fuses – standard practice in raids on industrial targets in Europe, in order to give workers time to get clear. The headquarters of the 3rd Bombardment Wing accordingly decided to mount a second operation against Ijmuiden on 17 May, although the commander of the 322nd, Colonel Robert M. Stillman, protested that another mission at low level against the same target was almost certain to end in disaster. HQ, however, was adamant; the mission had to be carried out, and Stillman had to do as he was told.

The group's senior intelligence officer, Major Alfred H. von Kelnitz, also believed that a second attack on Ijmuiden would be suicidal. On the morning of the projected attack he wrote a strong memo entitled 'Extreme Danger in Contemplated Mission', in which he pointed out that after the RAF raids of 2 and 5 May, as well as the 322nd's attack on the fourteenth, the Germans would be ready and waiting. 'For God's sake,' he pleaded, 'get fighter cover!'

Fighter cover was not available, however, and Lieutenant-Colonel Stillman, despite his misgivings, was forced to mount the attack without it. On the morning in question, 17 May, the group could only put up eleven serviceable Marauders. Six of these, led by Stillman himself, were to attack Ijmuiden, while the remaining five, led by Lieutenant-Colonel W.R. Purinton, carried out a diversionary raid on another power station in Haarlem.

The first Marauder lifted away from Great Saling at 10.56. The weather was perfect, with a cloudless sky and excellent visibility. The eleven aircraft formed up over the coast and headed out over the Channel at 50 ft (15 metres), keeping low to get under the enemy radar coverage. Then, with the Dutch coast only 30 miles (50 km) away, one of the marauders in the second flight experienced complete electrical failure and was forced to turn back. As it winged over on a reciprocal course, it climbed to 1,000 ft (300 metres) – just enough height to be picked up by the German coastal radar on the Dutch islands. The enemy now knew that a raid was coming in, and placed their fighter and AA defences on full alert.

The remaining aircraft flew on, making landfall a few minutes later. As they approached the coast, great geysers of water suddenly erupted in their path as heavy coastal guns opened up. Lashed by spray, the Marauders sped through the bursts and spread out into elements of two in order to present a more difficult target, increasing speed as they did so. As they crossed the coast, they were greeted by a storm of fire from weapons of every calibre, including rifles and machine-guns. The Germans had 20 mm and 40 mm multi-barrel flak guns emplaced among the sand dunes, and from these glowing streams of shells raced up to meet the bombers. There was no chance of evasive action; everything happened too quickly for that.

In the leading aircraft, Stillman opened up with his nose guns, watching his bullets churning up furrows of sand and stone as they converged on the gun position ahead of him. There was a brief, vivid impression of grey-clad figures throwing up their arms and collapsing, then he was kicking the rudder bar and yawing the Marauder to the left, his gunfire traversing the beach towards a second flak position.

The next instant, the world blew up in his face as a pattern of shells exploded all around the aircraft, knocking him momentarily senseless. The Marauder reared up, rolling uncontrollably, and Stillman came to just as it went over on its back. Out of the corner of his eye he saw his co-pilot, Lieutenent E.J. Resweber, slumped over the controls, either dead or badly wounded. Frantically, Stillman worked the controls, fighting to bring the Marauder back on an even keel. It was no use. The stick flopped uselessly in his hands; a shell had severed the control cables. The B-26 righted itself briefly, then went into another savage roll. Stillman looked up to see sand and scrub whirling past, a few feet from the cockpit canopy. He put his hands over his face. It was his last conscious action.

German soldiers on the beach threw themselves flat as the Marauder hurtled over their heads, its engines still howling. On its back, it smashed into the sand dunes at over 200 mph (300 kph), disintegrating in a great cloud of sand and smoke. Troops ran towards the debris, combing the wreckage for some sign of life. Miraculously, two men had survived the impact: Stillman and a gunner. Both men were badly knocked about, but they went on to recover in a German hospital.

Even as Stillman's aircraft was crashing, the flak was claiming more victims. Shells chewed into the starboard wing of Stillman's number two aircraft, and its pilot abruptly sheered off to the left to escape the line of fire, breaking right into the path of another B-26. There was a blinding flash, and suddenly the two machines were transformed into a ball of smoke and flame, shedding burning fragments as it rolled over and over towards the beaches. A third Marauder flew slap into the blazing cloud before its pilot had time to take avoiding action. Fragments slammed into it with the force of shrapnel; part of a wing dropped away and it spun down, out of control.

The wreckage of four out of six Marauders burned among the sand dunes. The two survivors of the first wave flew on bravely, intending to press home the attack, but a slight navigational error took them into the Amsterdam air defence zone and both were shot down by flak. Some crew members survived and were taken prisoner.

While the first wave was being massacred over the beaches, Lieutenant-Colonel Purinton's flight of four Marauders managed to slip through with only relatively light damage. The formation, however, was scattered all over the sky, and by the time some measure of cohesion was re-established the aircraft had wandered several miles off course. Vital minutes were lost while pilots and navigators searched for landmarks that would help them establish a new track to the target. Nothing was recognizable in the flat, featureless Dutch landscape. At last, Purinton decided to abandon what was fast becoming a fruitless and fuel-consuming quest and asked his navigator, Lieutenant Jeffries, for a heading home.

As the Marauders swung round westwards, Jeffries gave a shout. He had seen what he believed to be the target, away to the south-west. A minute later, there was no longer any doubt: the navigator had sighted Haarlem. The problem was that the crews had been briefed to hit the target from the south, where the AA defences were lightest. Now they would have to make the attack from the north-east, running the gauntlet of heavy flak.

Undeterred, Purinton decided to press on. With flak of every calibre rising to enmesh them from all sides they swept towards the outskirts of the town. The power station was ahead of them, just where the target maps and photographs had told them it would be. One of the Marauders in the second pair veered away sharply and dropped out of formation, trailing smoke. Its pilot dropped full flap, slid over a row of trees and stalled the bomber into a field. It bounced, shedding fragments, then slewed to a

stop. The crew scrambled out with no worse injuries than a few
bruises.

The other three Marauders roared over the power station and
dropped their bombs. Their bellies glittered palely in the sun as
they turned steeply to starboard, away from the murderous flak,
and sped low down for the coast. Shellfire raked Purinton's aircraft,
and with one engine chewed up by splinters and coughing smoke
he knew he had no chance of making it home. He retained just
enough control to slip over the coast and ditch the Marauder a few
hundred yards offshore. He and his crew were picked up a few
minutes later by a German launch. While they floated in their
dinghy, they saw another B-26 hit the water and cartwheel violently.
There were no survivors from that one.

Only one Marauder was left now. Its pilot, Captain Crane, pushed
the throttles wide open and headed flat out for the open sea. He
was too late. The Marauder's rear guns hammered as three
Messerschmitt 109s came streaking down from above and behind.
The fighters split up, one pair attacking from either flank and the
third aircraft racing towards the bomber head-on. The Marauder
was flying at only 150 ft (45 metres) but the Messerschmitt was
lower still, its slipstream furrowing the sea. It opened fire and shells
tore into the bomber's belly.

At the last moment the 109 climbed steeply, shooting past the
Marauder and stall-turning to come down on the bomber's tail for
the kill. The Marauder's tail gunner went on firing in short, accurate
bursts, seeing his bullets strike home on the fighter's mottled
fuselage. The 109 sheered off abruptly and headed for the shore,
losing height. Its last burst, however, had set fire to one of the
Marauder's engines, and Crane could no longer maintain height.
He made a valiant effort to ditch the aircraft in one piece, but it
bounced heavily and broke up, the fuselage plunging under the
surface like a torpedo. Only the flight engineer and rear gunner
managed to get out. They found a dinghy bobbing among the

A heavily flak-damaged B-26 struggles back to its base in East Anglia. (USAF)

A direct flak-hit rips the starboard engine out of the wing of a B-26.
(USAF)

islands of wreckage and pulled themselves aboard. It was to be their
uncomfortable home for four days before they were picked up by
a friendly vessel, the only survivors of the raid to come home.

Back at Great Saling, the 322nd's ground crews assembled at the
dispersals and peered into the eastern sky for a sign of the

returning aircraft. The first machine should have been back at 12.50 but that time came and went and the tension grew as the minutes ticked away. Half an hour later, with the telephone lines buzzing as operations room staff rang other airfields to see if any Marauders had made emergency landings, everyone knew the grim truth. Not one of the bombers that had set out was coming back.

Of the fifty-eight Americans who had set out on the mission, twenty-eight were dead. Twenty more, many of them wounded, were prisoners of the Germans, and two were safe. Stillman had been right: the raid had ended in disaster. But not even he had dreamed that it would be as bad as this. There was another factor, too, of which Stillman and the others had been unaware when they took off on the mission: on the previous night, 16/17 May, Lancasters of No. 617 Squadron, RAF Bomber Command, had breached the Möhne and Eder Dams in the Ruhr valley. The Lancasters' route had taken them across Holland, and the German AA defences there were naturally still jumpy. The news of the dams raid, however, was not released by the Air Ministry until the afternoon of 17 May, after damage assessment photographs had been examined.

There was one immediate result of the 17 May disaster: no more low-level attack missions were flown by the Marauders in the European theatre. All subsequent operations were carried out at medium level, and the Marauder went on to become one of the most successful and hard-worked of all Allied medium bombers.

In September 1944 the 322nd Bombardment Group moved to France in the wake of the D-Day invasion, and operated from bases on the Continent until the end of the war. It returned to the United States in November 1945, and was deactivated in December.

CHAPTER ELEVEN

The Raid That Failed

I n the summer of 1943, as the Allies consolidated their hold on Sicily and prepared to thrust across the Straits of Messina to gain a foothold on the Italian mainland, plans were laid for a strategic bombing attack which, it was hoped, would deal a crippling blow to the German war effort. The target was the Ploesti oil refinery complex near Bucharest, Romania, which supplied the bulk of the Axis' oil and petrol. Five bombardment groups of the US Ninth Army Air Force – the 44th, 93rd, 98th, 376th and 389th, all equipped

Consolidated B-24 Liberators in flight. The B-24's long range enabled it to strike at distant targets, albeit without fighter protection. (Author's collection)

with Consolidated B-24 Liberators – were to take part in the mission, flying from bases in North Africa. Three of the groups, the 44th, 93rd and 389th, were detached from the Eighth Army Air Force, based in the United Kingdom, and were under the temporary control of the Ninth AAF. Arriving during the last week in June, the Liberators were called upon to fly several missions against Italian targets – mainly communications, in support of the Allied invasion of Sicily. The last two weeks of July were devoted to training, the crews carrying out dummy attacks on targets deep in the desert.

When the UK-based Liberator groups arrived in North Africa, only a handful of people as yet knew the true nature of the mission, although crews speculated that it might involve low-level work because the advanced Norden bombsights had been removed from the aircraft and replaced by a more rudimentary type which was actually a modified gunsight. Extra bomb-bay fuel tanks were also fitted, indicating that it was to be a long-range mission.

The B-24 Liberator seemed to be the ideal aircraft to carry out the Ploesti raid. Powered by four 1,200 hp Pratt & Whitney radial engines, the big twin-finned bomber had a range of well over 2,000 miles (3,000 km), considerably longer than that of its contemporary, the B-17 Flying Fortress, and could carry a normal bomb load of 5,000 lb (2,250 kg). It carried a crew of twelve and a formidable defensive armament of ten 0.5 in machine-guns. In fact, a force of Liberators had already set out to attack Ploesti once before, in 1942, but that mission had been flown in darkness and poor weather and the bombers had returned to North Africa without locating the target.

It was apparent that, if the Liberators were to achieve a major success, the mission would have to be flown in daylight. No one denied that it would be highly dangerous, but the route to the oil refineries was thought to be lightly defended and the mission's low-level nature should, with luck, give the bombers a suffecent element of surprise to enable them to get through to the target without suffering too heavily.

The mission, code-named Statesman, was scheduled for Sunday, 1 August 1943. It was under the overall command of Major-General Lewis Hyde Brereton, commanding general of the Ninth AAF, and he left the crews in no doubt that their task would be attended by considerable peril. 'We expect our losses to be 50 per cent,' he told them, ' but even though we should lose everything we've sent, but still hit the target, it will be well worth it.'

The statement was not exactly calculated to raise the morale of the crews. From that moment on, many began to resign themselves to the probability that they were not going to come back from Ploesti.

Take-off on 1 August began at 07.10. The first group to get airborne was the 376th, based at Benghazi, Libya, and led by Colonel Keith K. Compton; next came the 93rd under Colonel Addison Baker; then the 98th from Benina under Colonel John Kane. It was here that the mission suffered its first setback, when one of the 98th's aircraft suffered engine failure on take-off and crashed while attempting a forced landing, killing all but two of its crew. The last two groups to take off were the 44th, led by Colonel Leon Johnson, and Colonel Jack Wood's 389th. In all, 179 heavy bombers were despatched.

Eleven aircraft aborted for various technical reasons not long after take-off. The remainder of the five groups flew on over the Mediterranean. Suddenly, at 09.50, completely without warning and for no apparent reason, the leading aircraft of the 376th Group – carrying the Group Navigation Officer, Captain Anderson – went into a steep climb, stalled and spun into the sea. The other Liberators began to straggle, their pilots confused as to who should take over the lead, and because of the strict radio silence there was no way, other than lamp signals, of passing the necessary information. In the end Colonel Compton's Liberator, which was also carrying General Uzal Ent, Chief of the Ninth Air Force Bomber Command, moved into the lead position. Because of the relative inexperience of Compton's navigator, Compton and General Ent assumed the navigation task for the group.

At 12.20, as the Liberators crossed Albania and were approaching Yugoslavia, they began to run into cloud, and the carefully planned tight formation, designed to afford the maximum defensive firepower, became dislocated as the groups lost sight of one another. The two leading groups, the 376th and 93rd, crossed the Romanian frontier on schedule and set course for their first turning point – Pitesti, some 60 miles (100 km) west of Ploesti – but the three following groups lost valuable time as they circled over the Danube, trying to get into some sort of order. When they eventually set course they were twenty minutes behind schedule.

The 376th and 93rd Groups, meanwhile, roared over the Romanian landscape at 200 ft (60 metres). As they flashed past Pitesti they came down even lower, leapfrogging trees and houses at heights as low as 30 ft (9 metres). The crews retained vivid

Shadow of a giant. A B-24 races at low level over the landscape en route *to its objective.* (Author's collection)

impressions of startled farmworkers in the fields. Some hurled themselves flat, while others stood their ground and hurled pitchforks at the speeding aircraft. One Liberator pilot had to pull up, quite literally, to avoid hitting a horse and cart, while others flew so low – perhaps inadvertently – that they found corn stalks jammed into crevices on the undersides of their aircraft on their return to base.

From Pitesti the Liberators were to steer due east, past Targoviste and on to Floresti. From there they were to turn south-east and follow the railway line to Ploesti. This route would enable them to approach the refineries from the north, and each crew had been briefed to pick out its individual target from this direction. When the two leading groups reached Targoviste, however, they sighted a railway leading south, and Compton and Ent decided that this was their turning point. Compton's young navigator protested that it was a mistake, but he was overridden by the general. So Compton's Liberator and sixty other aircraft turned to follow the line – which led not to Ploesti, but to Bucharest. It was only when the spires of the Romanian capital showed up ahead that Compton and Ent realized their mistake, but by then it was too late. The enemy flak batteries were alerted and hostile fighters were taking off from airfields all over the Balkans. Realizing that it was now futile to maintain radio silence, Ent told the other crews that he was making a left turn towards Ploesti. This would bring them up against the southern edge of the refinery complex, an approach angle on which none of them had been briefed.

Addison Baker's 93rd Group, in fact, had already realized their mistake and had turned back some minutes earlier; they would now be first over the target area. Meanwhile, the enemy defences were really getting geared up to hit the attacking bombers hard. At first, the Germans and Romanians had been puzzled when the Liberators were reported to be heading for Bucharest; they could not understand why the Americans should want to attack an innocent city which had no military value whatsoever. Then, when General Ent broke radio silence and the two leading bomber groups turned towards Ploesti, they knew the answer.

The three remaining groups, meanwhile, had reached Pitesti. As the 389th broke to port to make an individual attack on the refineries at Campina, 15 miles (25 km) north-west of Ploesti, the others flew on to Floresti and correctly turned on track for the target area. As they approached from the north, the 376th and 93rd groups were sweeping in on a converging course from the south, running the gauntlet of intense flak. With two large formations of bombers speeding towards one another at a closing speed of nearly 600 mph (950 kph), all flying at about the same height, the stage was set for disaster. As the 93rd and 376th groups reached the target area, enemy flak batteries laid a barrage in their path, filling the sky with every conceivable type of AA shell. Of the the 93rd Group, not more than five aircraft succeeded in bombing the primary target; the rest dropped their loads more or less at random over a wide area. The Liberator carrying the 93rd's commander, Lieutenant-Colonel Addison Baker, was shot down seconds after releasing its bombs; ten more aircraft of the group were destroyed over the target, one crashing into a women's prison.

While the 93rd was being shot to pieces, Compton had brought the 376th Group round in a wide 20-mile (30 km) semicircle to try to arrive over Ploesti from the correct angle. The flak, however, rose to meet them with incredible ferocity, and General Ent, realizing at last that the carefully laid attack plan had been torn to shreds, ordered the 376th's crews to attack whatever target they thought fit. This meant that the decision now rested on the shoulders of the group's five squadron commanders, each of whom led six

Liberators, and they were not slow to act. The CO of one squadron, Major Appold, selected the Concordia Vega installation and took his six Liberators roaring overhead, all releasing their bombs at the same time. The effect was spectacular, the oil storage tanks exploding in boiling flame and smoke. The Liberators emerged from the spreading black pall covered in soot, but otherwise unharmed. This, in fact, was the target that had been reserved for Addison Baker's 93rd Group.

Meanwhile, the 44th Group under Colonel Leon Johnson and the 98th led by Colonel John Kane were entering the target area from the north. The group commanders had no idea of the seriousness of the blunder that had been made until they saw several Liberators of the 376th Group flash past beneath them heading south-west, and observed that several of the targets earmarked for attack by the 44th and 98th had already been bombed. This meant that both groups had to fly directly into a holocaust of smoke and flame, running the risk of being destroyed in the explosions of delayed-action bombs. But there was no alternative; the Liberators bored in, the pilots steering blindly through sheets of flame that rose to heights of 500 ft (150 metres) and more. The great bombers were tossed aout the sky like corks in the fearsome turbulence; some pilots lost control and dived into the ground, others were incinerated in vast explosions as their fuel tanks blew up.

We all felt sick when we saw the oil tanks exploding,' commented one of the pilots who survived. 'Somebody ahead had bombed our target by mistake. There was nothing to do but try and hit it again; there was no time for another run on this trip.

One pilot of the 98th, Captain John Palm, saw the other five Liberators of his squadron go down in flames one after the other. He was the only one to reach the target, and as he approached it three of his engines were hit and knocked out. A second later a flak shell burst in the bomber's nose, killing two crew members outright and severing Palm's right leg. With his bomber losing height fast he managed to pull the emergency bomb release just in time. Then he slammed the Liberator down in a cornfield and dragged himself painfully out of the wreck through a cockpit window. Palm and several other crew members survived and were taken prisoner by the Romanians, who treated them well.

In theory, the easiest objective assigned to any group that day was the Steaua Romana refinery at Campina, the target of Jack Wood's 389th. Ground fire, however, proved exceptionally heavy, and a running battle developed between the Liberators' gunners and enemy machine-gun nests emplaced on the sides of hills. The bombers had to pass through a valley to reach their objective, and for a time they were so low that the enemy guns were firing down on them. One bomber, flown by Second Lieutenant Lloyd Hughes, was hit repeatedly and staggered on with white petrol vapour streaming from its ruptured tanks. As Hughes passed over the target and released his bombs, his aircraft passed through a sheet of flame which ignited the escaping fuel. With the whole of the port wing ablaze, Hughes tried desperately to make a forced landing, but the B-24 stalled and crashed. The whole sequence was captured by an official cameraman travelling on another B-24 – one of the most remarkable films to be shot during the Second World War.

Romanian IAR-80 fighters made repeated attacks on the Liberators as they left the target area. (Author's collection)

A few minutes later Campina was also hit by some Liberators of the 376th Group, searching for targets of opportunity.

The Liberators turned away on the first leg of the long flight back, the sky behind them dark with mushrooming smoke. It was now that the enemy fighters pounced on them: Focke-Wulfs and Messerschmitts of I/JG 4 under *Hauptmann* Hans Hahn, IV/JG 27 led by *Oberleutnant* Burk, and *Hauptmann* Lutje's IV/NJG 6. The Romanian Air Force was also engaged, flying a mixture of modern IAR-80 radial-engined fighters and a miscellany of older types, including a few Gloster Gladiator biplanes supplied to Romania by Britain in 1935. The latter proved more dangerous than expected, flying over the Liberators at top speed and dropping fragmentation bombs on them. Several bombers were reported to have been lost when these small but deadly missiles shattered their wings or tail units. As the Liberators flew south, they were also harried by Italian fighter squadrons.

At first the bombers were comparatively safe from serious attack. As long as they stayed at low level the enemy fighters found it difficult to engage them, but as soon as they climbed to cross the moutains the slaughter began. One by one the B-24s went down in flames, and as soon as one enemy fighter squadron broke off the action it was replaced by another. Precious fuel was used up as the American pilots took evasive action, with the result that few of the survivors managed to regain their North African bases. Some limped into Cyprus and Sicily; others made emergency landings in neutral Turkey, where their crews were interned.

The Ploesti raid brought the award of five Medals of Honor. One of them, posthumously, went to Lieutenant-Colonel Addison Baker, commander of the 93rd Group. After a shell struck the cockpit of Baker's bomber on the run-in to the target, injuring himself and his co-pilot, Baker had stuck rigidly to his course, even though a second heavy shell turned the Liberator into a mass of flame. He held control just long enough to get his bombs away, then apparently – according to eye-witness reports – tried to pull the stricken bomber up steeply so that the crew could attempt to bale out. Instead the Liberator began to somersault, like a giant blazing Catherine wheel, and dived into the ground with the loss of all on board. The eye-witnesses told how that last steep climb, with the Liberator in such a crippled condition, must have needed all the strength of two men pulling back on the control columns, so the inference was that Baker's co-pilot, Major John Jerstad, must have been helping. Jerstad was also awarded a posthumous Medal of Honor. So was the gallant young Lloyd Hughes of the 389th, who had made such a fierce attempt to save his crew after bombing Campina.

The fourth Medal of Honor recipient was Colonel Leon Johnson of the 44th, who, on finding that his assigned target had already been attacked, had stayed in the target area for some considerable time in search of another before finally setting course for home. Despite the severe damage inflicted on his Liberator, the *Suzy-Q*, Johnson brought her safely through to the Mediterranean with one other aircraft, Captain W.R. Cameron's *Buzzin' Bear*. These two Liberators were the only ones of the group's 66th and 67th Bombardment Squadrons, totalling seventeen aircraft, to regain their base at Benina. The others had either been shot down or had made emergency landings elsewhere.

For most of the returning crews, the long flight back over the Mediterranean was a nightmare. After being attacked by a strong formation of enemy fighters, the Liberator flown by Colonel Kane of the 98th Group had the housing around the propeller and three cylinders of its No. 4 engine shot to pieces and the propeller on the No. 1 engine shattered, the flying fragments slicing a hole in the aileron. To make matters worse, fuel was leaking from one of the wing tanks. The bomber staggered away from the target area on three engines, one of which was running roughly, and about 200 miles (300 km) south of the refineries the crew realized that they had no hope of making it back to North Africa. The navigator, Lieutenent Norman Whalen, therefore worked out a course for the nearest Allied airfield, which was on Cyprus.

Accompanied by two other damaged Liberators, Kane's bomber limped southwards at a few miles an hour above stalling speed. At one point it had to climb to cross a mountain range, so the crew threw out every movable object – oxygen bottles and masks, ammunition, radio and anything else they could dismantle – in an effort to reduce weight. They scraped through the mountains at 7,000 ft (2,100 metres), avoiding the higher peaks by flying through valleys. They landed in Cyprus at 21.10, exactly fourteen hours and forty minutes after they had left Africa that morning.

Others were not so lucky. One Liberator, flown by Lieutenant Gilbert Hadley and named *Hadley's Harem*, also tried to reach Cyprus with two engines out of action and two members of the crew killed by flak bursts. It got through the mountains safely, and was at 5,000 ft (1,500 metres) over the Aegean Sea when a third engine gave up the ghost. There was no alternative but to ditch, and as Hadley brought the aircraft down water poured into her through dozens of splinter holes in the fuselage, dragging her quickly under the surface. Hadley and his co-pilot were trapped in the cockpit and drowned; the seven survivors dragged themselves out of the wreckage with great difficulty and managed to reach the Turkish shore, which was less than a mile away.

As soon as they waded on to the beach they found themselves surrounded by Turkish peasants, armed to the teeth with ancient rifles, who built a huge fire and mounted guard all night while the exhausted Americans slept. The next morning, the airmen were resigned to the fact that they would shortly be interned when they were sighted by a low-flying RAF Wellington patrol aircraft. Within a short time an air-sea rescue launch arrived from Cyprus and the Americans were taken on board.

Crews who did manage to reach an Allied airfield, in North Africa or elsewhere, seemed numb with shock. White-faced and trembling with fatigue after their long ordeal, they told horrifying stories of Liberators crashing in flames over Ploesti, of great bombers smashed like matchwood into burning fragments, of blazing wreckage scattered across the contryside between the target area and the sea, of bombers exploding in mid-air over the refineries as they flew through soaring whirlpools of fire.

It was time to count the cost. Of the 179 Liberators dispatched on the raid, eleven had aborted and two had crashed, leaving 166 to attack the target. Of these, fifty-three had failed to return and most of the others were damaged. In human terms, 440 men were killed or missing, many others were wounded and about 200 were prisoners of war.

It was too high a price to pay, and the crews who did get back – together with many Americans in high places – were understandably eager to pin the blame on those who had planned the raid. The facts, however, were different. The attack plan had been good; the trouble was that it had relied too much on accurate timing, which was very difficult to achieve over such a distance even in the most favourable of conditions. It had also failed to take into account the extent of the enemy opposition. Even then, most of the casualties had been caused not by fighters but by intense ground fire, and with targets the size of Liberators flying only a few feet above the ground the enemy gunners had found it almost impossible to miss.

The planners were not to blame. Even though the attack plan had perhaps been over-ambitious and had placed too much confidence on the skill of the crews, it had certainly not been suicidal. Many factors had contributed to the fiasco, not least of which was the common USAAF practice of having a single lead navigator in charge of a formation with no adequate backup in case he was lost.

The disaster brought an effective halt to deep-penetration daylight missions over southern Europe by the USAAF until long-range escort fighters became available in 1944. There were to be more heavy raids on Ploesti that year, but on those occasions the bombers were operating from bases in Italy and escorted by long-range P-51 Mustang fighters. Yet the oil refinieries were never brought to a standstill; they were still producing oil when the Soviet Army rolled over them in August 1944.

CHAPTER TWELVE

The Anniversary Raids

In the summer of 1942 the first bombardment groups of the United States Eighth Army Air Force became operational on British bases. On 15 August 1942 twenty-four crews of the 97th Bombardment Group were alerted to carry out the first American bombing attack from Britain, with fighter cover provided by the Spitfire squadrons of No. 11 Group, RAF Fighter Command. After a delay caused by poor weather, the mission took place on 17 August, the target being the marshalling yards at Rouen. Twelve Boeing B-17 Flying Fortresses took part in the attack, with six more acting as a diversionary force along the French coast. The bombing, carried out in good weather conditions, achieved good results, and only one B-17 received slight flak damage. On 19 August two B-17s (out of twenty-four despatched) bombed the German fighter airfield at Abbeville; all returned safely to base. During the rest of the year the American daylight bombers, their forces steadily increasing, carried out many more attacks on targets in France and the Low Countries, all within range of fighter escort.

American plans to attack targets in Germany were delayed for a variety of reasons, mainly the lack of fighter escort and the Allied landings in North Africa, which helped to set back the Eighth Air Force's build-up in Britain because of the pressing need for heavy bombers in the Mediterranean theatre. But at the beginning of January 1943 General Ira C. Eaker, the Eighth AAF's commanding general, had 500 B-17s and Consolidated B-24 Liberators under his command, and he judged that the time was ripe for the big daylight offensive to begin. There was little doubt in the minds of the Allied commanders that 1943 would be the decisive year, the year in which the Allies, as the enemy was well aware, would attempt an invasion

The Boeing B-17 Flying Fortress, the aircraft that took the American daylight bombing offensive into the heart of Germany. (Author's collection)

of occupied Europe. Where the blow would fall no one yet knew, not even the Allies themselves, for the policy governing the conduct of the war in Europe at the close of the North African campaign had yet to be determined.

It was for this purpose that a top-level conference between President Roosevelt, Prime Minister Winston Churchill and the combined Allied chiefs of staff was held at Casablanca in January 1943. One of the decisions reached was to weld the strategic bombing arms of the RAF and USAAF into a single mighty weapon whose task would be, in the words of the resulting directive, 'the progressive destruction and dislocation of the German military, industrial and economic system, and the undermining of the morale of the German people to a point where their capacity for armed resistance is fatally weakened'.

The Americans believed that they could best fulfil the demands of the Casablanca Directive by carrying out concentrated daylight attacks on six principal target systems, designed to achieve the maximum destruction in selected major industries. These systems were, in order of priority: submarine construction yards and bases, the aircraft industry, the ball-bearing industry, oil production, synthetic rubber production and factories producing military transport. The target selected for the first American raid on Germany was one that fell within the leading category of objectives: the big naval base at Wilhelmshaven, a major centre of U-boat production. During the last week of January 1943 air reconnaissance revealed that the production yards were in full swing and that, as an additional bonus, the battleship *Admiral Scheer* was in dry dock.

On the morning of 27 January fifty-five B-17s took off from their English bases and set course over the North Sea. The weather was far from ideal for high-level precision bombing, and at altitude the cold was intense. The sub-zero temperatures knifed through the thickest flying clothing; machine guns, turrets and camera mechanisms froze, while windscreens and bomb sights were obscured by opaque layers of frost. One of the navigators described the outward flight:

At about 10.30 the altimeter indicated 25,000 feet [7,500 metres]. The cloud cover had ended, far below, and we could see the surface of the sea – like a sheet of glass. At 10.45 the Captain warned the crew to be extra alert. I looked out to the right and could see the outline of the coast of Germany and the row of islands that lay just off it. At 10.57 we were just over the islands and at 11.00 the tail gunner reported flak at six o'clock, below. It was from the coastal islands and was the first time we were fired on from German soil. At this time we were beginning to turn and we crossed the island of Baltrum and went into German territory. As we turned, the bombardier elevated the muzzle of his gun and fired a burst so that the tracers arched over into Germany. The first shots from our ship, Hell's Angel, *but not the last!*

The American raid took the German defences by surprise. Fifty-three Fortresses unloaded their bombs on the Wilhelmshaven harbour installations, opposed by only a handful of Focke-Wulf 190s; two more Fortresses bombed Emden. Only three B-17s failed to return, appearing to vindicate the Americans' belief that fears for the success of unescorted long-range daylight operations were unfounded. It would not be long before packs of determined *Luftwaffe* fighter pilots shattered the myth. In the days that followed the Wilhelmshaven mission, however, it was the weather and not the *Luftwaffe* that formed the main obstacle to the daylight bombing programme, with rain, sleet and dense cloud cover extending over the whole area of the North Sea. In seventeen days only one attack was carried out, in conditions of severe icing and sub-zero temperatures. The raid took place on 4 February, and the target was the port of Emden. Because of the freezing conditions dense contrails formed behind the American formation at a much lower altitude than usual, enabling the enemy fighters to concentrate on it without difficulty. Fifty fighters, including eight Me 110s of a night fighter unit, engaged the bombers over the north coast of Germany and a fierce air battle developed. Six Fortresses were shot down but the Germans also suffered heavily, losing eight fighters. On 16 February eight more bombers were lost during an attack on the locks leading to the basin of the St Nazaire U-boat base on the French coast. Ten days later another 8th Bomber Command formation battled its way through intense opposition to attack Wilhelmshaven for a second time. Seven bombers were lost. The end of one of them was described by *Leutnant* Heinz Knoke, flying a Messerschmitt 109 of II/JG 2.

I come in for a second frontal attack, this time from a little below. I keep on firing until I have to swerve to avoid a collision. My salvoes register this time. I drop away below. As I swing round I turn my head. Flames are spreading along the bottom of the fuselage of my Liberator. It sheers away from the formation in a wide sweep to the right.

Twice more I come in to attack, this time diving from above the tail. I am met by heavy defensive fire. My plane shudders under the recoil from the two cannon and the 13-millimetre guns. I watch my cannon shell-bursts rake along the top of the fuselage and right wing, and I hang on to the stick with both hands. The fire spreads along the right wing. The inside engine stops. Suddenly the wing breaks off altogether. The body of the stricken monster plunges vertically, spinning into the depths. A long black trail of smoke marks its descent. One of the crew attempts to bale out. But his parachute is in flames. Poor devil! The body somersaults and falls to the ground like a stone.

At an altitude of 3,000 feet [900 metres] there is a tremendous explosion, which causes the spinning fuselage to disintegrate. Fragments of blazing wreckage land on a farm 200 or 300 yards from the Zwischenahn airfield, and the exploding fuel tanks set the farm buildings on fire.

Despite the losses suffered in these early raids, it was decided early in March to carry out the first of 8th Bomber Command's deep-penetration missions against a German objective. On the 4th, four groups took off from their English bases to attack the big railway marshalling yards at Hamm, a target that had frequently been visited by the RAF. The operation was hampered by bad weather; two of the groups bombed the shipyards at Rotterdam, another returned to base with its bombs still on board, and only the 91st BG, consisting of sixteen bombers, reached the target. This lone group achieved an excellent bombing concentration, but four of its aircraft were shot down.

The next four missions were all against rail targets, including the marshalling yards at Rennes, hit by fifty B-17s on 8 March. Then, on the 18th, came the biggest raid so far, when ninety-seven heavy bombers – seventy-three Fortresses and twenty-four B-24 Liberators, the largest force that 8th Bomber Command had yet sent out to strike at one target – attacked the Vulcan shipbuilding yards at Vegesack, on the river Weser south of Bremen. The next day Wilhelmshaven was once again the target, followed in quick succession by the marshalling yards and repair shops at Rouen and the shipyards at Rotterdam. Eight bombers failed to return from these three missions, the last two of which were strongly escorted by Spitfires and Thunderbolts.

The next objective slated for a major attack by the Eighth Army Air Force was the Renault works, in the suburbs of Paris. This target, wrecked by RAF Bomber Command on the night of 3/4 March 1942, had been completely rebuilt by the Germans in nine months using French money and labour, and was now turning out

1,500 tanks and trucks per month for the Wehrmacht, which represented 10 per cent of the enemy's total production in this field. At 13.50 on 4 April 1943, eighty-five B-17s crossed Dieppe at 25,000 ft (7,500 metres) *en route* to Paris, clearly visible as a dark patch nestling in the loops of the Seine some 95 miles (150 km) to the south. At 14.00 the Spitfire escort turned back, at the limit of its combat radius, but as the Fortresses flew on unescorted there was still no sign of any enemy fighters; the *Luftwaffe* had been lured north by three diversionary attacks mounted by No. 2 Group RAF Bomber Command. At 14.14 the B-17s were over the target, and in the next seven minutes the groups dropped 251 tons of high explosive on it. Enemy fighters appeared for the first time as the bombers swung north towards the coast, and determined attacks persisted until the B-17s made rendezvous with more Spitfire squadrons over Rouen. Four bombers were lost, but reconnaissance showed that the Renault factory had once again been devastated.

The Eighth Air Force's raids continued to grow in size, and in human cost. On 17 April 115 B-17s took off to attack the Focke-Wulf aircraft factory at Bremen. Eight aborted, but the remaining 107 battled their way to the target through fierce opposition. Sixteen failed to return, making this the costliest mission so far for the Americans. By this time two factors – both by-products of the weather over western Europe – were beginning to hamper daylight operations to a noticeable extent. First of all, in early spring the days were still not long enough to permit the American crews – who were not trained for night operations – to attack targets in Germany outside a limited period midway between dawn and dusk. This period usually tended to coincide with maximum cloud development in the target area, so that visual identification of the target became a problem. Secondly, and for the same reason, the Germans were able to calculate the probable time of an American attack quite accurately and assemble their fighters accordingly. The latter needed to be on alert only from about three hours after sunrise to about three hours before sunset. The end result was that the Americans met with stronger opposition than ever during April and May 1943, and their losses rose to a serious level.

By the middle of May 1943 the Eighth Air Force had sufficient aircraft and crews operational in England to carry out a long-awaited experiment: simultaneous large-scale attacks on several targets. The first such mission took place on 14 May, when over 200 Fortresses and Liberators were despatched in the space of four hours to attack Ijmuiden, Antwerp, Courtrai and Kiel. The diversity of the

attacks caused some confusion among the German fighter
controllers; nevertheless, the *Luftwaffe* hotly contested the Kiel
attack, which was by far the biggest of the four, and six B-17s and
five B-24s were lost. Seventeen of the latter aircraft took part. Flying
at a lower level than the Fortresses, they were singled out for
concentrated attack. The pilot of one B-24 described the engagement:

> *Three of them started at us. Our top turret gunner picked out the leader
> and let him have about fifty rounds from each gun. The co-pilot saw
> black smoke pour from the nacelle and the plane go into a spin. Despite
> the temperature of 20 degrees below zero Centigrade I was sweating like
> mad. I had on a pair of winter flying boots and nothing else except
> regular dress, which was wringing wet.*
>
> *Two more fighters came in from the nose. I could see them firing their
> cannons, so I pushed forward on the stick with all my might. We went*

*Bombs rain down as a B-17 formation reaches its objective. Falling
bombs were always a hazard to bomber formations at the lower levels.*
(Author's collection)

down like a brick-built privy and they whizzed past us, barely missing the top of our wing. One of them took along several slugs with him, because our tracers were seen to go through his fuselage. When I pulled out of that dive, our top turret gunner was thrown from his turret, as was the tail gunner. All the other members of the crew were thrown about a bit. But the Jerries had missed us, and that was the important thing.

In June 1943 the Combined Chiefs of Staff issued their directive for the start of Operation Pointblank, the joint round-the-clock Anglo-American bombing offensive against Germany's war industries. In terms of offensive power the Eighth Air Force was well equipped to undertake such a mission; by the beginning of July its strength had increased to fifteen bomber groups comprising more than 300 B-17s and B-24s. The biggest obstacle to the success of deep-penetration daylight missions remained the lack of long-range fighter escort. In an effort to fill this critical gap the Americans slung drop-tanks under the wings of their Thunderbolts and Lightnings, which enabled them to penetrate as far as Germany's western frontier, but this did not provide a real solution. On 28 July 1943 Thunderbolts escorted seventy-seven Fortresses in two formations as far as the German frontier before turning back. The bombers flew on towards their targets: the Fieseler aircraft factory at Kassel-Bettenhausen and the AGO factories at Oschersleben, near Magdeburg. Enemy fighters engaged the B-17s from the moment they crossed the border, and one unit – II/JG 2 – employed a novel attack technique: its Messerschmitts flew at 3,000 ft (900 metres) above the bombers and dropped 500 lb (225 kg) bombs on them. Three bombers in one formation were destroyed by this means. The remainder scattered, and the Messerschmitts pounced. II/JG 2 alone destroyed eleven bombers, and the total American loss was twenty-two. Several other bombers were badly damaged,four of them so seriously that they were written off in landing accidents on returning to England.

During the last week of July 1943 the Eighth Air Force made five major sorties against sixteen major targets. The longest mission was a 1,900 miles (3,000 km) round trip to attack the German U-boat base at the Norwegian port of Trondheim. During seven days of operations 8th Bomber Command lost eighty-eight aircraft, mostly Fortresses. This intensive phase began with the Trondheim attack on 24 July; the next day the target was the Blohm und Voss shipyards at Hamburg, obscured by a pall of smoke from the massive fires started by RAF Bomber Command the night before.

At the same time other formations attacked the shipyards at Kiel and the *Luftwaffe* training school and airfield at Wustrow. Nineteen B-17s failed to return. On the 26th, the Fortresses struck at the Continental Gummiwerke AG, Hanover. They left the target in flames, with a massive mushroom of smoke rising to 20,000 ft (6,000 metres). Sixteen bombers were shot down, and eight more were destroyed over Hamburg and other secondary targets.

On 17 August 1943, the first anniversary of 8th Bomber Command's attack on Rouen in 1942, the Eighth Air Force mounted a maximum-effort strike on two nerve centres of the German aircraft industry, the Messerschmitt factory at Regensburg and the ball-bearing plants at Schweinfurt. This was literally to be a 'hit and run' attack on a massive scale, with a total of 376 B-17s involved. The Regensburg force was to fly on to airfields in North Africa, while the Schweinfurt force would return to England after its attack. What followed was the biggest air battle seen up to that time.

An eye-witness to it was Lieutenant-Colonel Beirne Lay, Jr, flying as an observer on the Regensburg attack with a crew of the 100th Bombardment Group. Based at Thorpe Abbots in Suffolk, the 100 BG, which had been operational since 23 June 1943, was to suffer such appalling losses during its combat career that it became known as the 'Bloody Hundredth'.

At 1017 hours, near Woensdrecht, I saw the first flak blossom out in our vicinity, light and inaccurate. A few minutes later, two Fw 190s appeared at one o'clock and whizzed through the formation ahead of us in a frontal attack, nicking two B-17s in the wings and breaking away beneath us in half rolls. Smoke immediately trailed from both B-17s, but they held their stations. As the fighters passed us at a high rate of closure, the guns of our Groups went into action. The pungent smell of burnt powder filled our cockpit, and the B-17 trembled with the recoil of nose and ball gun-turrets. I saw pieces fly off the wing of one of the fighters before they passed from view.

Here was early action. The members of the crew sensed trouble. There was something desperate about the way those two fighters came in fast right out of their climb without any preliminaries. Three minutes later the gunners reported fighters climbing up from all around the clock, singly and in pairs, both Fw 190s and Me 109s. Every gun from every B-17 in our Group was firing, criss-crossing our patch of sky with tracers. Both sides got hurt in this clash, with two Fortresses from our low squadron and one from the Group ahead falling out of formation on fire with crews baling out, and several fighters heading for the deck in flames with their pilots lingering behind under dirty yellow parachutes. I noticed an Me 110 sitting out of range on our right. He was to stay with us all the way to the target, apparently reporting our position to fresh squadrons waiting for us down the road. At the sight of all these fighters I had the distinct feeling of being trapped. The life expectancy of our Group suddenly seemed very short, since it appeared that the fighters were passing up the preceding Groups in order to take a cut at us.

Swinging their yellow noses round in a wide U-turn, a twelve-ship squadron of Me 109s came in from twelve o'clock in pairs and in fours, and the main event was on. A shining silver object sailed over our right wing. I recognized it as a main exit door. Seconds later, a dark object came hurtling through the formation, barely missing several props. It was a man, clasping his knees to his head, revolving like a diver in a triple somersault. I didn't see his 'chute open.

A B-17 turned gradually out of the formation to the right, maintaining altitude. In a split second, the B-17 completely disappeared in a brilliant explosion, from which the only remains were four small balls of fire, the fuel tanks, which were quickly consumed as they fell earthwards. Our airplane was endangered by falling debris. Emergency hatches, exit doors, prematurely opened parachutes, bodies, and assorted fragments of B-17s and Hun fighters breezed past us in the slipstream.

I watched two fighters explode not far beneath, disappearing in sheets of orange flame, B-17s dropping out on every state of distress, from engines shot out to control surfaces shot away, friendly and enemy parachutes floating down, and, on the green carpet far behind us, numerous funeral pyres of smoke from fallen fighters, marking our trail. The sight was fantastic: it surpassed fiction.

On we flew through the strewn wake of a desperate air battle, where disintegrating aircraft were commonplace and sixty 'chutes in the air at one time were hardly worth a second look. I watched a B-17 turn slowly out to the right with its cockpit a mass of flames. The co-pilot crawled out of his window, held on with one hand, reached back for his chute, buckled it on, let go, and was whisked back into the horizontal stabilizer. I believe the impact killed him. His 'chute didn't open.

Ten minutes, twenty minutes, thirty minutes, and still no let-up in the attacks. The fighters queued up like a bread line and let us have it. Each second of time had a cannon shell in it. Our B-17 shook steadily with the fire of its .50s, and the air inside was heavy with smoke. It was cold in the cockpit, but when I looked across at the pilot I saw that sweat was pouring off his forehead and over his oxygen mask. He turned the controls over to me for a while. It was a blessed relief to concentrate on holding station in formation instead of watching those everlasting fighters boring in. It was possible to forget the fighters. Then the top turret gunner's muzzles would pound away a foot above my head, giving a realistic imitation of cannon shells exploding in the cockpit, while I gave an even better imitation of a man jumping six inches out of his seat.

A B-17 of the Group ahead, with its right Tokyo tanks on fire, dropped back to about 200 feet above our right wing and stayed there while seven of the crew successively baled out. Four went out the bomb bay and executed delayed jumps, one baled from the nose, opened his 'chute prematurely and nearly fouled the tail. Another went out the left waist gun opening, delaying his 'chute opening for a safe interval. The tail gunner jumped out of his hatch, apparently pulling the ripcord before he was clear of the ship. His 'chute opened instantaneously, barely missing the tail, and jerked him so hard that both his shoes came off. He hung limp in the harness, whereas the others had shown immediate signs of life after their 'chutes opened, shifting around in the harness. The B-17 then dropped back in a medium spiral and I did not see the pilots leave. I saw it just before it passed from view, several thousand feet below us, with its right wing a sheet of yellow flame.

After we had been under constant attack for a solid hour, it appeared certain that our Group was faced with annihilation. Seven of us had been shot down, the sky was still mottled with rising fighters, and it was only 11.20 hours, with target-time still thirty-five minutes away. I doubt if a man in the Group visualized the possibility of our getting much further without one hundred per cent loss. I know that I had long since mentally accepted the fact of death, and that it was simply a question of the next second or the next minute. I learned first-hand that a man can resign himself to the certainty of death without becoming panicky. Our Group firepower was reduced thirty-three per cent; ammunition was running low. Our tail guns had to be replenished from another gun station. Gunners were becoming exhausted.

One B-17 dropped out of formation and put its wheels down while the crew baled out. Three Me 109s circled it closely but held their fire, apparently ensuring that no-one stayed in the ship to try for home. Near the IP, at 11.50 hours, one hour and a half after the first of at least 200 individual fighter attacks, the pressure eased off, although hostiles were still in the vicinity. We turned at the IP at 11.54 hours with fourteen B-17s left in the Group, two of which were badly crippled. They dropped out soon after bombing the target and headed for Switzerland.

Weather over the target, as on the entire trip, was ideal. Flak was negligible. The Group got its bombs away promptly on the leader. As we turned and headed for the Alps, I got a grim satisfaction out of seeing *a rectangular column of smoke rising straight up from the Me 109 shops. The rest of the trip was a marked anticlimax. A few more fighters pecked at us on the way to the Alps. A town in the Brenner Pass tossed up a lone burst of futile flak. We circled over Lake Garda long enough to give the cripples a chance to rejoin the family, and we were on our way towards the Mediterranean in a gradual descent. The prospect of ditching as we approached North Africa, short of fuel, and the sight of other B-17s falling into the drink, seemed trivial matters after the vicious nightmare of the long trip across southern Germany. We felt the reaction of men who had not expected to see another sunset. At 18.15 hours, with red lights showing on all the fuel tanks in my ship, the seven B-17s of the Group which were still in formation circled over a North African airdrome and landed. Our crew was unscratched. Sole damage to the airplane: a bit of ventilation around the tail from flak and 20 mm shells. We slept on the hard ground under the wings of our B-17, but the good earth felt softer than a silk pillow.*

For the 8th Bomber Command the ordeal of 17 August 1943 was not yet over. In the early afternoon 229 Fortresses crossed the Dutch coast *en route* to bomb the ball-bearing factories at Schweinfurt. On this occasion determined fighter attacks began as soon as the formation reached German territory. The *Gruppen* attacked in pairs, one engaging the Allied fighter escort and the other the bombers. At times more than 300 German fighters were in the air, and fierce battles raged along the route to the target. The fighter attacks intensified after the Americans' P-47 escort turned for home; thirty-six Fortresses were shot down, bringing 8th Bomber Command's total loss for the day to sixty bombers. Over 100 more were damaged, many of them so severely that they had to be scrapped.

After this mauling it was to be five weeks before the American heavy bombers carried out any more long-range missions over Germany. General Eaker, however, was determined to sustain the daylight offensive, and early in October it was judged that the Eighth Air Force was ready to resume its deep-penetration attacks; but when they started again, the lessons of August were rammed home even more forcibly. During one week, between 8 and 14 October, when the Americans attacked Bremen, Marienburg, Danzig, Münster and once again Schweinfurt, they lost 148 bombers and nearly 1,500 aircrew. On the Schweinfurt raid, on 14 October, which became known as Black Thursday, the *Luftwaffe* flew over 500 sorties and destroyed sixty of the 280 bombers taking part – over 20 per cent.

Group Captain J.E. 'Johnnie' Johnson, commanding a formation of Spitfires heading out into the Low Countries to escort the returning bombers, described the aftermath of this terrible encounter.

It was a clear afternoon, and we first saw their contrails many miles away, as well as the thinner darting contrails of the enemy fighters above and on either flank. As we closed the gap we could see that they had taken a terrible mauling, for there were gaping holes in their precise formations. Some Fortresses were gradually losing height, and a few stragglers, lagging well behind, were struggling to get home on three engines.

We swept well behind the stragglers and drove off a few 109s and 110s, but the great air battle was over, and what a fight it must have been, because more than half the bombers we nursed across the North Sea were shot up. One or two ditched in the sea, and many others, carrying dead and badly injured crew members, had to make crash-landings. How we longed for more drop tanks, so that some of the many hundreds of Spitfires based in Britain could play their part in the great battles over Germany.

The North American P-51 Mustang, the aircraft that established Allied air superiority over Europe in 1944. (Author's collection)

With the Eighth Air Force reeling from this succession of disasters and RAF Bomber Command beginning to suffer increasingly heavy losses at the hands of the German night fighter force, the prospect for the combined Allied air offensive looked grim. In the RAF's case, a solution would soon come in the shape of the long-range Mosquito night-fighter, which would patrol the flanks of the night bomber streams and stalk its enemy counterparts; but for the American daylight bombers, the problem was different. What was needed here was a fighter with sufficient fuel to escort the B-17s and B-24s all the way to the target, engage the enemy fighters in combat, and have enough fuel remaining to escort the bombers home again. Such an aircraft, the North American P-51 Mustang, was already in service with the RAF in the tactical reconnaissance role, and in November 1943 the first USAAF Mustang unit, the 354th Fighter Group, established itself at Boxted, near Colchester in Essex, where it came under the operational control of the Eighth Air Force. It was the first of many, and the superb Mustang – eventually fitted with a Packard-built Rolls-Royce Merlin engine – was without doubt the aircraft that went on to win the daylight battle over Europe.

CHAPTER THIRTEEN

Mosquito Mission

The thirtieth day of January, 1943, was a very special day for Adolf Hitler. Exactly ten years earlier, he had brought the Nazi Party to power in Germany, and embarked on the path of rearmament and expansion that was to lead inexorably to war.

The Nazis had planned big celebrations to mark this tenth anniversary. There was to be a huge military parade in Berlin, and Hitler himself would make a radio broadcast at 11.00. The propaganda minster, Josef Goebbels, would make another speech at 16.00.

There would be no celebrations in Stalingrad, where the German Sixth Army, surrounded by Soviet forces, exhausted and starving, freezing in the Russian winter, was entering its final days. Nor was there cause for celebration in North Africa, where German and Italian forces, trapped between two Allied armies, were about to make a futile last stand in Tunisia.

At 08.30, with the military parade already starting to assemble in Berlin, Hitler sat at breakfast and waded through the mound of telegrams that had flooded in from the party faithful all over Germany. Unknown to the *Führer*, however, one present had yet to arrive. It would be delivered in exactly two and a half hours' time, by the RAF.

The Germans had made no secret of their anniversary celebrations. Although Berlin had been raided many times at night, they did not believe that the RAF had an aircraft capable of striking at the capital by daylight and surviving its flak and fighter defences.

They were wrong. Five hundred miles (800 km) from Berlin, three sleek aircraft were running up their engines on the RAF airfield at Marham, in Norfolk. They were twin-engined de Havilland Mosquitoes, the RAF's newest and fastest bombers. The Mosquito bomber had entered service with No. 105 Squadron just over a year earlier, and had already carried out several daring attacks on enemy targets. Now, on this January morning, No. 105 Squadron was about to take the war into the very heart of the Third Reich.

Although No. 105 Squadron had received its first Mosquito B.IVs in November 1941, the need to develop a special version of the standard 500 lb (225 kg) bomb, enabling four to be fitted into the aircraft's bomb bay, had resulted in a considerable delay before the type could be declared operational, so the next six months were spent in training; any operational flying being carried out by the Blenheims which the squadron retained during this working-up period. The first operational sortie by the squadron's Mosquitoes was flown in the early morning of 31 May, when four aircraft led by Squadron Leader A.R. Oakeshott made a daylight attack on Cologne, devastated by the first 1,000-bomber raid the night before, while a fifth was despatched in the late afternoon to make a low-level reconnaissance flight over the city. One of the Mosquitoes was shot down by flak and crashed in the North Sea, its two-man crew losing their lives.

No. 105 Squadron, now fully established with Mosquitoes, continued to despatch small numbers of aircraft on operations while its crews built up experience; two aircraft were sent to Essen on 2 June 1942, and both returned safely. On 25/26 June, four Mosquitoes were part of a 1,000-bomber force that attacked Bremen, and in the weeks that followed 105 Squadron's aircraft visited Essen and Kiel. No. 139 Squadron also began to receive Mosquitoes in July, and on the 2nd it despatched six aircraft to make a low-level attack on U-boat construction yards at Flensburg. The attack was led by Squadron Leader Oakeshott, now commanding No. 139 Squadron, who was shot down by fighters; he and his navigator, Flying Officer V.F.E. Treherne, were killed. A second aircraft crashed after being hit by flak over Flensburg and crashed in Germany, its crew being taken prisoner. This attack was an exception, as Mosquitoes were generally despatched singly to different targets during this period.

On 22 September 1942, four Mosquitoes of No. 105 Squadron led by Squadron Leader D.A.G. Parry, DSO, DFC, took off from RAF Leuchars in Scotland to attack the Gestapo HQ in Oslo. The raid was timed to coincide with a rally of 'Quisling' Norwegians who supported the Germans. As they attacked in pairs, racing at low level along Oslo Fiord, the Mosquitoes were intercepted by three Focke-Wulf 190s, one of which hit the aircraft flown by Flight Sergeant Carter and set it on fire. Carter headed for neutral Sweden, pursued by the Focke-Wulf, but crashed in a lake. The others hit the Gestapo building with four bombs and made their escape. Three of the bombs passed straight through the building before exploding; the fourth stayed inside, but failed to explode. Nevertheless, the attack was a huge propaganda success, and it was only now that the Mosquito was revealed to the public. One of the Focke-Wulfs crashed near Oslo, killing its pilot and giving rise to strong rumours that the Mosquito bombers were armed, which they were not.

Also during this period, the Mosquito bomber squadrons refined their tactics. Daylight attacks were carried out by two waves of aircraft, both of which would make their approach to the target at low level to avoid detection by enemy radar, the crews navigating by dead reckoning. While the first wave swept over the target at low altitude, concentrating the fire of the defences on itself, the second wave popped up to 1,500 or 2,000 ft (450–600 metres) to make a fast diving attack, followed by a low-level getaway. These tactics were used successfully on 27 January 1943, when Wing Commander H.I. Edwards, VC, led nine Mosquitoes of Nos 105 and 139 Squadrons in a raid on the submarine Diesel engine works in the shipbuilding yards of Burmeister and Wain at Copenhagen. The 1,400 mile (2,250 km) round trip strained the Mosquitoes' endurance to the utmost, loaded as they were with 500 lb (225 kg) bombs, and for two hours it was heavy going through banks of cloud and rain over the North Sea. There was one early casualty; shortly after crossing the enemy coast the Mosquitoes encountered heavy flak, and Flight Lieutenant J. Gordon called out that he had been hit. Blue smoke was pouring from his starboard wing and he naturally jumped to the conclusion that the flak had caused some damage. In fact it was not flak, but Gordon felt justified in taking violent evasive action, in the course of which he flew through some telegraph wires, damaging his port wing. He made it back to base.

Over the target the weather improved, and conditions were perfect as, with dusk falling, Edwards led his aircraft over the Danish capital at heights of between 50 and 300 ft (15–90 metres), the pilots dodging the chimneys and many spires of Copenhagen as they made for the island east of the city, where the shipyards stood. There was intense flak now, from both shore batteries and ships in the harbour, and the Mosquitoes were so low that they had to jink to avoid the tops of masts. At 17.05 the first bombs were away; they had delays ranging from eleven seconds to thirty-six hours, and all the bombers managed to hit the target area. As they turned away they noticed a huge fire, with flames shooting 100 ft

(30 metres) into the air. Enemy fighters were on the alert now, but with their bomb loads gone the Mosquitoes were too fast for them. It was a shell from an AA gun on the Danish mainland that shot down one Mosquito, flown by Sergeant Dawson, while another flak-damaged aircraft, piloted by Sergeant Clare, struggled back to England only to crash as it was attempting an emergency landing near Shipdham. Six Mosquitoes of the original nine returned to base, having been in the air for five hours and thirteen minutes.

Three days later, three Mosquitoes of No. 105 Squadron delivered the Nazi Party's birthday present.

As they roared away from Marham and set course for the German capital, Squadron Leader Bob Reynolds, the raid leader, was conscious that everything depended on split-second timing. The plan was to bomb the Berlin radio station, just off the Wilhelmstrasse, at exactly 11.00, to coincide with the start of Hitler's speech. Reynolds' navigator, Pilot Officer E.B. Sismore, was one of the best, and needed to be. Apart from the question of timing, the five-hour round trip would leave only a small margin of fuel. There was no room for error, or for a great deal of evasive action if they were attacked.

The Mosquitoes raced across the North Sea at low level, climbing slightly as they crossed the German coast. The morning was brilliantly clear, and Sismore had no trouble in picking out landmarks as the bombers sped on. Reynolds climbed hard now, taking the three aircraft up to 20,000 ft (6,000 metres) for their final run towards the target. The lakes around Berlin came up under the nose, metallic patches glistening in the sunshine. In Britain, linguists monitoring the German radio shortly before eleven o'clock heard an announcer tell the audience to stand by for an important speech.

Then came the blow. The speech was to be made not by Hitler, but by the *Luftwaffe* Commander-in-Chief, *Reichsmarschall* Hermann Göring. Hitler, it appeared, had developed a sore throat earlier that morning, and Göring was standing in for him. The only consolation was that Göring was the most important person in Germany after the *Führer*.

The Mosquitoes were over Berlin now. With thirty seconds to go, Sismore centred the broad ribbon of the Wilhelmstrasse in his bombsight. A few tufts of scattered flak burst around the speeding aircraft, but there was no sign of any fighters.

All over Germany, millions of people listened to their radios as a fanfare of trumpets died away and the announcer began to introduce Göring's speech. Suddenly, the words were cut short. Clearly, over the radio, came the heavy crump of exploding bombs as the 500-pounders dropped by the three Mosquitoes whistled down to erupt around the broadcasting station. There was a long pause, punctuated by sounds of confused shouting in the background. Then, breathlessly, the announcer said that there would be some delay. His voice faded out and was replaced by martial music. It was nearly an hour before Göring eventually came on the air. He was clearly harassed and angry. Only a few years earlier, he had boasted that no enemy aircraft would ever fly over the territory of the Reich. Now the RAF had visited the Reich's capital in broad daylight.

All three Mosquitoes returned safely to base – but for the RAF, the day's work was not yet over. At 12.35 three more Mosquitoes, this time drawn from No. 139 Squadron and led by Squadron Leader D.F.W. Darling, also took off from Marham. They flew at wavetop height to a point north of Heligoland, then turned in towards Lübeck. By this time the weather had deteriorated, and the aircraft ran through squalls along the whole of their route. The German defences were on the alert, as the attackers soon discovered.

As the Mosquitoes climbed up to 20,000 ft (6,000 metres) Sergeant R.C. Fletcher, the navigator in the number two aircraft, shouted a warning: Messerschmitt 109s were attacking from astern. Fletcher's pilot, Sergeant J. Massey, and Flight Sergeant P.J. McGeehan, who was flying the third aircraft, both took violent evasive action and managed to shake off the fighters. Squadron Leader Darling was not so lucky. He was last seen diving down into cloud, apparently out of control, and he failed to return from the mission.

The two remaining Mosquitoes flew on above a dense cloud layer. At 15.55 they arrived over Berlin and Sergeant Massey dropped his bombs through a gap in the clouds. By this time the flak was intense, and it was another eight minutes before Flight Sergeant McGeehan could get into position to make a successful bombing run. His bombs burst half a mile south of the city centre. Their noses down to gain speed, the two bombers raced for the coast evading the worst of the flak and the fighters that rose to intercept them. They landed safely at Marham at 18.30. Goebbels' speech went out on time – from the safety of an underground bunker.

On 1 June 1943, Nos 105 and 139 Squadrons were assigned to No. 8 (Pathfinder) Group, joining another Mosquito squadron, No. 109. In December 1942 this unit had pioneered the use of the blind bombing and target marking system known as Oboe, in which two ground stations transmitted pulses to an aircraft, which then received them and retransmitted them. By measuring the time taken for each pulse to go out and return, the distance of the aircraft from the ground stations could be accurately measured. If the distance of the target from station A was known, the aircraft could be guided along the arc of a circle whose radius equalled this distance. The bomb release point was calculated and determined by station B, which 'instructed' the aircraft to

A de Havilland Mosquito FB. Mk.VI prepares to depart on a mission over occupied Europe. (Author's collection)

release its bombs when the objective was reached. This meant that targets could be attacked through cloud. The Mosquito strength of No. 8 Group eventually reached a total of eleven squadrons.

The major Mosquito variant was the FB Mk.VI fighter-bomber, which in addition to its internal bomb load was armed with a battery of four 20 mm cannon and four 0.303 in machine-guns in the nose. In its low-level day bomber role, operating with the squadrons of No. 2 Group, the Mosquito VI was a spectacular success in its attacks on precision targets, such as power stations and headquarters buildings. The first tactical Mosquito VI formation was No. 140 Wing, based initially at Sculthorpe in Norfolk and comprising Nos 464 (RAAF), 487 (RNZAF) and 21 (RAF) Squadrons; the second was No. 138 Wing, which formed at Lasham in Hampshire in December 1943 with Nos 107, 305 (Polish) and 613 Squadrons. In the early months of 1944 No. 2 Group's squadrons carried out some daring and much publicized 'pinpoint' attacks before becoming part of the 2nd Tactical Air Force and moving to the continent in the autumn to support the Allied advance through north-west Europe.

In February 1944, in what was to be remembered as one of the most famous low-level attacks of all time, aircraft of No. 140 Wing, commanded by Group Captain Percy Pickard, bombed and breached the walls of Amiens prison, allowing over 200 French prisoners, many of them Resistance fighters, to escape. The RAF initially had qualms about the attack, which was laid on at the request of the French Resistance, because it would almost certainly result in civilian casualties. Six crews from each squadron were selected to make the attack, code-named Operation Renovate. The day fixed for the attack, 18 February 1944, dawned overcast and grey, with squalls of sleet sweeping across the wing's base at Hunsdon, Hertfordshire. The forecast indicated that the route to the target would also be covered by heavy, low cloud. Nevertheless, it was decided that the attack was to go ahead, as many of the French prisoners were in danger of imminent execution. The raid was to be led by No. 487 Squadron. At noon precisely, three Mosquitoes were to blast a hole in the eastern wall of the prison, and three minutes later, three more aircraft would bomb the northern wall. No. 464 squadron would then make its attack, one section of three aircraft bombing the south-eastern corner of the prison while the other section attacked the north-eastern wing. The third squadron, No. 21, was to remain in reserve in case any of the other attacks failed.

The three squadrons began taking off at 11.00 in a snowstorm, each aircraft carrying a pair of 500 lb (225 kg) bombs with eleven-second delayed-action fuses. The Mosquitoes made rendezvous with their fighter escort, three squadrons of Typhoons, over Littlehampton, and headed out over the Channel. Despite the poor visibility, Amiens proved easy to locate and the Mosquitoes skirted the town to the north, heading for their target along the straight, poplar-lined Amiens–Albert road. The New Zealand squadron attacked on schedule at 12.01, just as the German guards were sitting down to lunch, bombing from as low as 50 ft (15 metres), and the bombs of the leading aircraft struck the eastern wall about 5 ft (1.5 metres) above ground level.

Meanwhile, the second section of three aircraft made its approach from the north. Wing Commander R.W. Iredale, leading the first section of No. 464 Squadron, later described the attack:

From about four miles away I saw the prison and the first three aircraft nipping over the top. I knew then it was OK for me to go in. My squadron was to divide into two sections, one to open each end of the prison, and it was now that one half broke off and swept in to attack the far end from the right. The rest of us carried on in tight formation. Four hundred yards before we got there, delayed-action bombs went off and I saw they had breached the wall. Clouds of smoke and dust came up, but over the top I could still see the triangular gable of the prison – my aiming point for the end we were to open. I released my bombs from 10 ft and pulled up slap through the smoke over the prison roof. I looked around to the right and felt slightly relieved to see the other boys still 200 yards [182 metres] short of the target and coming in dead on line. They bombed and we all got away OK, re-formed as a section, and made straight for base.

Meanwhile, Pickard, who had gone in with the Australians, now broke off to act as master bomber. He flew low over the prison, examining the damage, and only when he was satisfied that all the objectives had been attained did he order the Mosquitoes of No. 21 Squadron to set course for home, their bombs still on board. As the aircraft left the target area, one of them – a No. 464 Squadron aircraft flown by Squadron Leader I.E. McRitchie – was hit by light flak and went down out of control. Pickard immediately turned back to fly over the wreck, presumably to see what had happened to the crew. His Mosquito was caught by Focke-Wulf 190s and shot down; he and his navigator, Flight Lieutenant Alan Broadley, were killed. All the other aircraft returned safely to base.

And the walls came tumbling down … The raid on Amiens prison captured by the cameras of one of the attacking Mosquitoes. (Author's collection)

Grp Captain Percy Pickard, who lost his life in the Amiens raid, pictured in the cockpit of a Miles Messenger communications aircraft. (Author's collection)

Of the 700 prisoners in Amiens, 255 escaped when the walls were breached, although 182 of them were later recaptured. Thirty-seven prisoners died during the raid, though that total includes some who were shot by guards as they attempted to escape. Fifty German guards were killed.

Two months later, in what an Air Ministry bulletin described as 'probably the most brilliant feat of low-level precision bombing of the war', the Mosquitoes attacked the Gestapo headquarters at The Hague, the nerve centre of German operations against the resistance movements in the Low Countries. It was a 90 ft (25 metres) high five-storey building tightly wedged among others in the Schevengsche Weg, and was strongly defended by light anti-aircraft weapons. The task of destroying the building was assigned to No. 613 Squadron, commanded by Wing Commander Bob Bateson. A scale model was built, perfect in every detail, right down to the thickness and composition of the walls. Alongside the planners, scientists worked hard to develop a new bomb, a mixture of incendiary and high explosive, that would have the maximum destructive effect on the Gestapo's stored files and records. Bateson picked his crews carefully, and put them to the test during several weeks of intensive training. The raid was scheduled for 11 April 1944, Bateson leading six Mosquitoes from Lasham, Hampshire.

As they approached The Hague the Mosquitoes split up into pairs. Flight Lieutenant Peter Cobley, following in line astern behind Bateson, saw his leader's pair of bombs drop away and literally skip through the front door of the HQ. Cobley dropped his own bombs in turn, pulling up sharply over the roof of the building. The other four aircraft made their attacks at short intervals, all their bombs hitting the target, which was completely destroyed with very little collateral damage.

On 31 October 1944, another Gestapo headquarters, this time at Aarhus in Denmark, was attacked by twenty-five Mosquitoes of No. 140 Wing, led by Wing Commander Bob Reynolds. The mission was flown from Thorney Island, the Mosquitoes carrying a total of thirty-five 500 lb (225 kg) delayed-action bombs. Fighter escort was provided by eight Mustangs. The HQ was located in two adjoining buildings that had previously formed part of the University of Aarhus; once again, the Mosquito crews were faced with the problem of making an effective attack while causing the minimum of damage to civilian property. They did so brilliantly, leaving the headquarters shattered and ablaze. More than 200 Gestapo officials were killed in the attack, and all the files on the Danish resistance movement were destroyed in the fire. One Mosquito actually struck the roof of the building, losing its tailwheel and half its port tailplane. Despite the damage; it flew home – testimony to the aircraft's ruggedness.

On 31 December 1944, Mosquitoes of No. 627 Squadron carried out an equally successful attack on the Gestapo HQ at Oslo, and on 21 March 1945 it was once again the turn of the three squadrons of of No. 140 Wing, when Bob Bateson led them in a daring low-level attack on the main building of the Gestapo HQ in Copenhagen. Although the target was completely destroyed, the success of the mission was tragically marred when one of the Mosquitoes, striking an obstacle with its wingtip, crashed on a convent school and killed eighty-seven children. The scale of the tragedy was compounded by the fact that the end of the war in Europe was so near. But it must be set against the wider picture of total war, with all its evils; a war in which the Mosquito played a memorable part in bringing about the final Allied victory.

CHAPTER FOURTEEN

Last Strikes by the *Luftwaffe*

By the middle of 1944, the *Luftwaffe* was no longer master of the European sky. Its resources spread out on three fronts, it was being relentlessly ground down under the weight of the Allied air offensive. Yet, weakened though it was, in the last year of the war it demonstrated on more than one occasion that it was still capable of striking hard and with devastating effect.

Since December 1943, negotiations had been in progress between the US and Soviet governments for the use of Russian bases by Allied aircraft, principally B-17s. Known as Project Frantic, this scheme would enable American bombers operating out of England or Italy to bomb selected targets on the outward trip, land in Russia to refuel and rearm, then attack other targets on the way home. As a secondary aim, it was hoped that these 'shuttle-bombing' missions would force the *Luftwaffe* to disperse its already overstretched resources still further in an effort to meet the new attacks over a larger strategic area that included German-occupied Polish territory.

It was not until April 1944 that the Russians agreed, and even then they allocated only three airfields instead of the six required. All three lay in the devastated 'scorched earth' area around Kiev, and throughout April and May 1944 American engineers laboured to extend runways, build new base facilities and generally get the fields into shape. Of the three, only Poltava was really suitable for handling heavy bombers; Mirgorod could accommodate only a few, while Piryatin was just big enough to be used by fighters.

Project Frantic was eventually launched on 2 June 1944, when thirty B-17s and seventy Mustangs of the Fifteenth Army Air Force took off from their Italian bases, bombed the marshalling yards at

Debrecen and flew on to the airfields in Russia. From there, on 6 June, they struck at the airfield of Galatz in Romania; and on the 11th, on their way back to Italy, they also bombed the Romanian airfield at Foscani. Only two B-17s and two Mustangs were lost in these three operations. On 21 June it was the turn of the Eighth Air Force, which for some weeks had been totally committed to tactical operations in support of the Normandy landings. By the middle of the month the situation on the ground was well under control, and strategic attacks on targets deep inside Germany were resumed. One of the principal targets was Berlin, and as the main force approached the enemy capital a smaller group of 114 B-17s broke away and bombed a synthetic oil plant at Ruhland,75 miles (120 km) further south. Escorted by seventy P-51s, this force then flew on towards the 'Frantic' airfields around Kiev, which were reached late that afternoon. Seventy-five B-17s landed at Poltava; the rest touched down at Mirgorod, while the Mustangs assembled at Piryatin.

What the American crews did not know was that, as they flew high over eastern Europe, they had been shadowed by a lone Heinkel He 177 long-range bomber. As darkness fell, eighty Ju 88s and He 111s of General Rudolf Meister's IV *Fliegerkorps*, based on airfields in southern Russia, took off and headed for the Ukraine, led by He 111 'illuminators' of *Kampfgeschwader* 4. Before the night was out, the Americans were to learn to their cost that the *Luftwaffe* was still capable of striking fast and hard.

At 23.35 Russian authorities warned the American HQ staff at Poltava that enemy aircraft had crossed the front line and were reported to be headed for the Kiev area. The alert was sounded and the Allied personnel on the three 'Frantic' airfields took cover. Thirty minutes passed; nothing happened and the tension began to ease a little. Then, a few minutes after midnight, there was a sudden roar of engines over Poltava and clusters of flares cascaded down, dropped by the Heinkel He 111s of KG 4. The Flying Fortresses, only one of which was camouflaged, were clearly visible. Then the first bombs fell, and for an hour Poltava was pounded by the Heinkels and Junkers 88s of three *Kampfgeschwader*, the aircraft attacking singly from medium altitude. The last wave, consisting entirely of Ju 88s, swept over the field at low level, raking it with cannon and machine gun-fire.

When the last of the bombers departed, the airfield at Poltava was littered with the wrecks of forty-seven B-17s, and every one of the remaining twenty-six bombers had suffered damage. Nearly half a million gal (2.25 million litres) of petrol had gone up in flames. Several Russian and American fighters and two C-47 transports had also been destroyed. The enemy bombers had dropped 100 tons of bombs; not a single aircraft had been lost. The Poltava disaster, taken together with the casualties suffered by 8th Bomber Command in action over Germany earlier that day, represented an overall loss of ninety-one aircraft – the highest ever sustained by the Americans in a single day's operations. Twenty-four hours later the *Luftwaffe* tried to repeat this success in an attack on Mirgorod, but by that time the Americans had gone. Never again would the *Luftwaffe*'s dwindling bomber force achieve so much in a single blow. As for Operation Frantic, the shuttle-bombing tactics continued on and off for the next two months before being dropped for good.

Four months later, at dawn on New Year's Day, 1945, the *Luftwaffe* launched Operation *Bodenplatte* ('Baseplate'), a massive attack on Allied airfields in Belgium, Holland and northern France by about 800 fighters, led by Ju 88 night fighters and bombers acting as pathfinders. One group came in over the Zuider Zee to strike at Brussels-Evere, another attacked Eindhoven – both airfields being occupied by the RAF Second Tactical Air Force – and the third flew past Venlo to hit the airfields occupied by the US Ninth Tactical Air Force. The whole operation was intended to relieve pressure on the German offensive in the Ardennes, which had begun on 16 December 1944 and which had now stalled and, as the weather began to clear, was coming under increasing air attack.

The plan was not popular with the German pilots involved. *Oberleutnant* Willi Heilmann, commanding IV/JG 54 based at Varrelbusch between Achmer and Oldenburg, and equipped with the 'long-nose' Focke-Wulf Fw 190D-9, later wrote:

> *It was not an enviable task. The pilots had fallen into a deep depression owing to the continued successes of the British and Americans, and there was a growing conviction that the outcome of the war had already been decided ... Sixty Fockes took off in the grey twilight. In this snowstorm a long period of circling over the airfield was necesssary until all the machines were in a good formation position. The order came through from the ground station: 'Course 180'. Nothing else. This should have given me an inkling that something out of the ordinary was under way. No weather report and no target ...*
>
> *Visibility was so bad that we naturally had to fly in bad weather formation. The squadrons flew behind each other in order to avoid*

collision, and at this low altitude we were taking our lives in our hands, for the hilltops of the Teutoberger Wald were covered with cloud. Slowly the twilight enveloped the countryside ... Windscreen wipers began to hum as they swept the snow from the windscreens. I could see about five machines around me; the rest were enveloped in snow and cloud and mist. As we were flying so low, we were unable to make radio contact with ground control, and the situation was chaotic. We did not know where we were going or what we were supposed to do.

This was on 31 December 1944, New Year's eve. After flying in deteriorating weather for some time, Heilmann recognized the Mitteland Canal and was able to fix his position. He led his aircraft down to land at nearby Rheine-Hopsten airfield in the semi-darkness. To his amazement, he discovered that his group had actually been meant to land at Hopsten; the destination airfield was to have been passed to the pilots by ground control once they were airborne, but control had failed to establish contact.

Early the next morning, the pilots were briefed on the forthcoming mission.

Brussels was the target for our fighter wing. The formations were to fly in close consecutive waves led by fast pathfinders over the North Sea and then to make a wide sweep to port until they reached the Dutch coast. After that they would have to find their own directions, for by that time it would be light enough. The whole mission was to be carried out at less than 600 feet [180 metres] until we reached the targets, so that the enemy ground stations could not pick us up. To this end, radio silence was the order until we reached the target. Machine after machine took off, circled and regrouped. Squadron after squadron set out. Far ahead the navigating lights of the leading pathfinders twinkled in the early dawn.

Things went off as planned. Over the sea the pathfinders turned off to the left and the squadrons flew round on to a southern course. But the addle-pated High Command had forgotten one thing – or else they had purposely omitted it on security grounds – they had not notified their own anti-aircraft. Although the fighters fired their own recognition flares, a crazy flak barrage claimed its first victim over the coast.

My squadron was in the first wave. The calm of a New Year's morning still lay over the sleeping city of Brussels as we flew in and made for our target – the big airfield of Haren. It was crammed with aircraft, as we could see at once. Long rows of uncamouflaged four-engined bombers, for the most part Boeings, stood on the airfield. On the opposite side of the field to the north were scores of fighters ... Within five minutes the whole airfield, with aircraft, fuel tanks, workshops and buildings, had been turned into a smouldering scrap-heap. In pyjamas, vests and pants, the gunners had rushed to their positions. In a panic, pilots and ground staff, many of them bare-foot rushed through the snow and tumbled head over heels into any spot of cover they could find...we winged our way homewards at low level.

Operation *Bodenplatte* had achieved complete surprise, and almost 300 Allied aircraft were destroyed – but the success was wiped out by a comparable German loss, made even more tragic for the *Luftwaffe* by the fact that about 200 of the attacking fighters were shot down by their own flak when they passed through an area which was thick with V-2 rocket-launch batteries and consequently heavily defended. Among the dead German pilots were fifty-nine experienced fighter leaders. What had been conceived as a brilliant operation had therefore turned into an appalling disaster from which the *Luftwaffe* never recovered.

Volkel, which was occupied by the Hawker Tempest Mk V fighters of the RAF's No. 122 Wing, escaped almost unscathed

The cost of Operation Bodenplatte *was high. Here, a Focke-Wulf 190 falls to the guns of an Allied fighter.* (Author's collection)

The formidable Hawker Tempest Mk V was the most powerful Allied piston-engined fighter of the Second World War. (Author's collection)

because of navigational errors and was attacked by only four or five Messerschmitt 109s. Many of No. 122 Wing's Tempests were out on armed reconnaissance when the attack developed at 09.00. The only squadron still at base, No. 80, was quickly scrambled for airfield defence and Flying Officer Garland, leading Red Section, shot down two Fw 190s which were intercepted at treetop height. The other Tempest squadrons, returning home short of ammunition, nevertheless attacked several German fighters which were sighted leaving the target area and shot six of them down, also claiming one probable and four damaged.

The biggest challenge facing the Allied air forces in Europe during the closing months of the war was the Messerschmitt Me 262 jet fighter-bomber, which carried out many hit-and-run missions during the Allied advance through north-western Europe and was extremely difficult to counter. Design work on the Me 262, the world's first operational jet fighter, began in September 1939, a month after the successful flight of the world's first jet aircraft, the Heinkel He 178, but because of delays in the development of satisfactory engines, the massive damage caused by Allied air attacks and Hitler's later obsession with using the aircraft as a bomber rather than a fighter, six years elapsed between the 262 taking shape on Messerschmitt's drawing board and its entry into *Luftwaffe* service. Because of the lack of jet engines the prototype Me 262V-1 flew on 18 April 1941 under the power of a Jumo 210G piston engine, and it was not until 18 July 1942 that the Me 262V-3 made a flight under turbojet power. December 1943 saw the first flight of the Me 262V-8, the first of the type to carry a full armament of four 30 mm MK 108 cannon. By the end of 1944 730 Me 262s had been completed, and a further 564 were built in the early months of 1945, making a total of 1,294 aircraft. The Me 262 initially went into production as a pure fighter, entering service with a trials unit known as *Erprobungskommando* 262 (EK 262) at Lechfeld, near Augsburg, in August 1944.

The Me 262 presented a serious threat to Allied air superiority during the closing weeks of 1944. Two versions were now being developed in parallel: the Me 262A-2a *Sturmvogel* ('Stormbird') bomber variant and the Me 262A-1a fighter. The *Sturmvogel* was issued to *Kampfgeschwader* 51 'Edelweiss' in September 1944; other bomber units that armed with the type at a later date were KG 6, 27 and 54. There were also two reconnaissance versions, the Me 262A-1a/U3 and Me 262A-5a.

The Me 262s began to appear in growing numbers in the autumn of 1944, carrying out fast low-level attacks on Allied installations

A Messerschmitt Me 262A-2a Sturmvogel, *the fighter-bomber version of the jet.* (Author's collection)

and armoured columns. Although a number had been destroyed by Allied fighters when No. 122 Wing rearmed with Tempests, such successes were usually a matter of luck, because no Allied fighter came anywhere near to matching the Me 262's speed. The latest mark of Spitfire, the Griffon-engined Mk XIV, was hopelessly outclassed in terms of speed, as is illustrated in this report by Flight Lieutenant Jim Rosser of No. 66 Squadron. Rosser was patrolling over Venlo at 15,000 ft (4,500 metres) one day in September 1944 when he sighted an Me 262 a few thousand feet lower down.

> *I don't think any of our chaps had actually managed to shoot down a 262 at that time, and I thought this was my big chance. I went down after him, flat out, but he saw me coming and opened up the taps. Smoke trails streamed from his turbines and off he went; I hadn't a hope in hell of catching him, so I gave up and rejoined the formation.*
>
> *The incident had an interesting sequel. Years after the war, when I was stationed in Germany, I met a colonel in the Federal German* Luftwaffe. *We had a few drinks and got talking, and it turned out that*

The Me 262 was an aerodynamically graceful design. Its drawback was its Jumo 004 turbojets, which had a life of only 25 hours. (Author's collection)

> *he had flown 262s. We compared dates, places and times, and by one of those extraordinary coincidences it turned out that he had almost certainly been the pilot of 'my' 262. He said that if I had kept after him, it was on the cards that I would have got him. His fuel was very low, and he couldn't have maintained full throttle for more than half a minute.*

Volkel was a tempting target for the Me 262s, which usually managed to slip through the patrolling fighter screen and the flak belt to scatter anti-personnel bombs across the airfield. In October 1944 the base was host to no fewer than fourteen fighter squadrons, being shared by the Tempests of No. 122 Wing, the Typhoons of No. 121 Wing and the Spitfires of No. 126 (RCAF) Wing. No. 121 Wing was the worst affected by the marauding jets, suffering a considerable number of casualties, whereas No. 122 Wing had only one man killed.

The Me 262s' hit and run tactics were not confined to ground attack operations; they were also used to good effect in attacks on Allied bomber formations. They were very active during February 1945, with US Eighth Air Force bomber crews reporting 163 encounters with the jets and escorting Mustang pilots 118. Most of the 262s belonged to the newly formed JG 7 'Hindenburg' *Geschwader*, commanded by *Oberst* Johannes Steinhoff. Although JG 7 eventually comprised three *Gruppen*, only one of these, III/JG 7, made real and continual contact with the enemy, moving in turn to bases at Brandenburg-Briest, Oranienburg and Parchim.

Attacks were usually made by units of *Staffel* (squadron) size, consisting of nine aircraft in three elements of three, employing the 'vic' formation with one aircraft leading and the other two on the flanks, slightly higher up and to the rear. If more than one *staffel* was used the others flew on both sides to the rear and slightly higher, or to one side in echelon. Because of the jets' high speed there was no need for top cover. Once the bomber formation had been sighted, each *Staffel* commander selected an individual bomber group, beginning the attack run from a distance of 5,000 yards (4,600 metres) and 5,000 ft (1,500 metres) higher up. On the approach, the basic three-aircraft elements of the *Staffel* went into line astern, diving to a point some 1,500 ft (450 metres) below and 1,500 yards (1,370 metres) behind the bombers to gain speed before pulling up and flying straight and level for the last 1,200 yards (1,100 metres). On the last stage of the attack the 262s reached a speed of about 530 mph (850 kph), more than enough to avoid the Allied fighter escort.

In addition to the 262's normal Revi gunsight, which was used in conjunction with the fighter's 30 mm cannon, each aircraft had gradations etched on its windscreen, spaced so as to frame the wingspan of a B-17 at a range of 650 yards, at which point a salvo of R4M rockets was launched. (III/JG 7 received its first batch of these unguided 55 mm missiles, twenty-four of which could be carried on underwing racks, in mid-February 1945.) When the salvo was fired it spread out rather like a charge of shotgun pellets, increasing the chances of hitting one or more targets. Immediately the rockets were discharged the 262 pilot would open up with his cannon, closing in to 150 yards (137 metres) before breaking off. Taking full advantage of the 262's high speed, the German pilots would sweep low over the top of a bomber formation in a flat climb, either attacking a second formation or diving away if the Allied fighter escort was too close for comfort. Pilots were discouraged from flying underneath the bomber formation after an attack, as there was a danger of debris being sucked into the jet intakes. Since the 262's endurance was strictly limited, the pilots usually headed for home after one firing pass.

The enemy jet activity in February 1945 began on the 9th, when about twelve Me 262s attacked a bomber formation in the Fulda area, north of Frankfurt. Mustang pilots claimed four kills and one probable. The Mustangs claimed three more 262s on 22 February, when the Allied air forces carried out Operation Clarion, a major attack on enemy marshalling yards, but the really big day for the

US VIII Fighter Command came on the 25th, when the Mustang pilots destroyed no fewer than eight Me 262s and one Arado 234 jet bomber.

The Arado 234 and seven of the Me 262s, were destroyed by pilots of the 55th Fighter group during a fighter sweep in the vicinity of Giebelstadt airfield. Two of the 262s were destroyed by Captain Donald Cummings, as his combat report reveals.

> I was leading Hellcat Yellow Flight on a fighter sweep at 10,000 feet in the vicinity of Giebelstadt airdrome when several Me 262s were called in at nine o'clock, taking off from the field. Captain Penn, the squadron leader, ordered us to drop our tanks and engage the enemy.
>
> I peeled off from 11,000 ft, making a 180 degree turn to the left in a seventy degree dive after a jet which was then approaching the airdrome. I commenced firing from approximately 1,000 yd (914 metres) in a steep, diving pass and after about three seconds observed many strikes. Since I was closing fast and approaching the airfield, which was beginning to throw up intense and accurate flak, I broke left and up, taking evasive action when about one-third of the way across the field. My wingman, who was behind me, saw the E/A touch ground, cartwheel and burn.
>
> During the above engagement my number three and four men had become separated from the flight, so my wingman and I set out on a course of 180 degrees at 5,000 ft in search of ground targets. Near Leipheim a/d we spotted an unidentified aircraft crossing the south-west corner of the field at 4,000 ft; 150 degrees. We increased our speed and closed on the E/A which we identified as an Me 262 with dark camouflage and large crosses on its wings. As I came in range, the jet made a sharp turn to the left, losing altitude. When I followed him, closing slowly, he started to let down his nosewheel, apparently intending to land. Closing further to 400 yd (366 metres), I commenced firing. The first burst missed, but when the jet attempted to turn to the right I gave it to him again at about ten degrees deflection and observed many strikes. Large pieces of the E/A began to fly off and the fuselage exploded below the cockpit. The 262 then rolled to the right and went straight in from 800 ft, exploding as it went.

The Ar 234 *Blitz* ('Lightning'), mentioned above, was the world's first operational jet bomber. The origins of the type went back to a 1940 requirement issued by the German Air Ministry for a fast, turbojet-powered reconnaissance aircraft. The prototype Ar 234V-1, which flew for the first time on 15 June 1953, and the next seven aircraft (Ar 234V-2 to V-8) all used the trolley-and-skid launching and landing arrangement. The second prototype, the Ar 234V-2, was similar in all respects to the first machine, but the Ar 234V-3 was fitted with an ejection seat and rocket-assisted take-off equipment, the rocket pods being installed under the wings.

Although the launching trolley and landing skid arrangement had functioned well, it was realized that the aircraft's immobility on landing would be a severe disadvantage when it came to operational deployment, so it was decided to abandon this configuration and with it the Ar 234A-1, as the initial production version was to have been designated, and fit the aircraft with a conventional wheeled undercarriage. The fuselage was slightly widened to accommodate two mainwheels midway along its length, and a nosewheel was mounted under the pilot's cockpit. In this guise the aircraft was designated Ar 234B, of which 210 were built. Only two versions were used operationally; these were the Ar 234B-1 unarmed reconnaissance variant, and the Ar 234B-2 bomber. It was planned to replace the B series in production by the C series, but only nineteen production Ar 234C-3 bombers had been completed when the war ended.

The first operational Ar 234 sorties were flown by the V-5 and V-7 prototypes, which were delivered to I/*Versuchsverband.Ob.d.L* (*Luftwaffe* High Command Trials Unit) at Juvincourt, near Reims, in July 1944. Both aircraft were fitted with Walter rocket-assisted take-off units and made their first reconnaissance sorties on 20 July, photographing harbours on the south coast of England from an altitude of 29,500 ft (9,000 metres). Several more sorties were made over the UK before the unit was transferred to Rheine in September. Other reconnaissance trials units received the Ar 234, and in January 1945 these were amalgamated into I/F100 and I/F123 at Rheine, and I/F33 at Stavanger, Norway. The latter unit flew reconnaissance sorties over the British naval base at Scapa Flow, in the Orkneys, until mid-April 1945.

The bomber version of the Ar 234 equipped *Kampfgeschwader* 76 from October 1944, flying its first operational missions during the Ardennes offensive in December. The jet bombers were very active in the early weeks of 1945, and from 7 to 17 March 1945 they joined Me 262 fighter-bombers in carrying out a ten-day series of attacks on the Ludendorff bridge at Remagen, which had been captured by the Americans.

Enemy jet fighter activity reached an unprecedented level in March 1945, and this was sustained throughout most of April. In these two months, USAAF fighters alone reported 438 encounters, resulting in 280 combats with claims of forty-three Me 262s destroyed in the air, three probably destroyed and forty-five damaged, together with twenty-one destroyed and eleven damaged on the ground.

Meanwhile, authority had been given for the formation of a second Me 262 jet fighter unit. Known as *Jagdverband* 44, and commanded by Lieutenant-General Adolf Galland, it comprised forty-five highly experienced pilots, many of them Germany's top-scoring aces. Its main operating base was Munchen-Riem, where its main targets were the bombers of the Fifteenth Army Air Force, coming up from the south, while JG 7 continued to operate from bases in northern and central Germany. On 7 April 1945, JG 7 demonstrated the Me 262's remarkable potential when it took on the American fighter escort and destroyed twenty-eight P-47 Thunderbolts and P-51 Mustangs; but there was no escaping the fact that on that same day, the *Luftwaffe* lost 183 piston-engined Messerschmitt 109s and Focke Wulf 190s in what was the last series of major air battles over Germany.

Three days later, over 1,000 American bombers launched massive attacks on the *Luftwaffe*'s jet fighter bases. The 262s shot down ten bombers, but with their bases devastated they were compelled to withdraw to airfields as far afield as Prague, the jet units broken up and scattered piecemeal. In the last days of April the remnants of JV 44 moved still further south to Salzburg, but the jets were grounded through lack of fuel. Most of the 262s were destroyed by their ground crews shortly before the airfield was overrun by American tanks on 3 May.

Of the total of almost 1,500 Me 262s produced before the end of the war, less than a quarter saw combat. Had the figure been higher, the jets would certainly have inflicted severe punishment on the American daylight formations – and probably on the RAF's night bombers too, for the 262's potential as a night fighter was belatedly recognized. As the Allies advanced deeper into Germany, they found plenty of evidence of the devastating weapon the Me 262 might have become. Time and again, during the early days of May 1945, they came upon rows of jet fighters parked in the pine forests that bordered bomb-cratered *autobahns*, together with stockpiles of R4M rockets, all awaiting delivery to *Luftwaffe* units that no longer existed.

CHAPTER FIFTEEN

Intruders

In mid-May 1940, in the wake of the German *Blitzkrieg* in France and the Low Countries, RAF Bomber Command began operations for the first time against oil and communications targets in Germany, having hitherto confined itself to fringe attacks directed mainly against naval facilities. Such raids, mounted in growing strength, were intolerable to the Nazi leadership and in particular to *Reichsmarschall* Hermann Göring, the *Luftwaffe* C-in-C, who had earlier boasted that if enemy bombs ever fell on the Reich territory people might call him Meier – a predominently Jewish name.

It is untrue that the *Luftwaffe*'s pre-war planners had given no thought to the night defence of Germany. Even before the war, a Messerschmitt 109 squadron at Greifswald was assigned to night-fighting practice with the aid of searchlights, and a specialist night fighter unit, 10/JG 26, also equipped with Bf 109s, was on the order of battle in September 1939, although it was very much experimental. The unsuitability of the Bf 109 for night-fighter operations quickly became apparent, and following the start of the RAF's strategic offensive the first effective night-fighter units were formed, equipped in the main with Bf 110s. In addition to these, a specialist long-range night-fighter unit, I/NJG 2, was also established with three squadrons of Junkers Ju 88s and one of Dornier Do 17s. Tasked with long-range night-fighter operations, this was the *Luftwaffe*'s first night intruder *Gruppe*, and early in August 1940 it deployed forward to Gilze-Rijn in Holland, from where it began operations against the British Isles in September under the command of Hauptmann Karl-Heinrich Heyse.

The *Gruppe*'s operational area over Britain was divided into three sectors. Sector One covered an area bounded by the Thames estuary, northern London, the east Midlands and the Wash, taking in the whole of East Anglia; Sector Two ran inland from the Wash to

Birmingham, then swung north to Sheffield and north-east to the Humber, covering Lincolnshire and south Yorkshire; while Sector Three ran from the Humber to Sheffield, Sheffield-Leeds, Leeds-Blackpool and finally from Blackpool to a point on the Northumbrian coast north of Newcastle upon Tyne. This was the only sector to extend as far as the west coast and was the largest in area – although by no means the most important, as the other two encompassed the two areas where Bomber Command had its densest concentration of airfields.

After some preliminary sorties over Lincolnshire in late August and September 1940, the intruders brought their war to the northernmost sector on 21 September, when *Hauptmann* Karl Hulshoff destroyed a Whitley of No. 58 Squadron, the aircraft crashing near Thornaby with the loss of all four crew. Three nights later, *Feldwebel* Hans Hahn shot down a 102 Squadron Whitley near Linton-on-Ouse. In the early hours of 28 September Lindholme was attacked by *Leutnant* Heinz Volker, who damaged a Hampden of No. 49 Squadron as it was landing and shot down a second just off the coast.

During this initial period of operations the intruders lost four aircraft, although only one is thought to have been destroyed by the air defences – in this instance by anti-aircraft fire. During October and November the sortie rate was low, but in December several sorties were flown against the Lincolnshire airfields, in the

Much use was made of the Dornier Do 17 in early Luftwaffe *intruder operations. Here, a shot-down example is examined by RAF personnel.* (Author's collection)

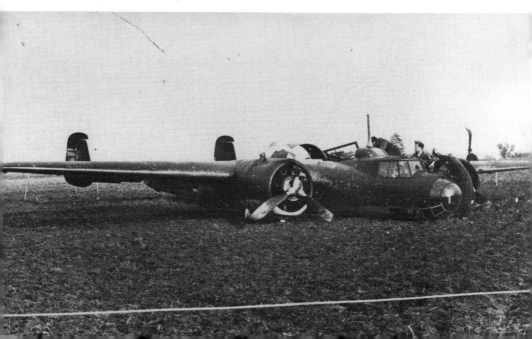

course of which a Dornier 17 was destroyed and another damaged by Hurricanes of No. 12 Group flying night patrols. During one of these sorties, the *Gruppe* commander, Major Karl-Heinrich Heyse, was shot down and killed by the Manby airfield defences.

Meanwhile, Fighter Command had been compelled to adopt what might best be described as desperate measures to counter the enemy night raiders, for the *Luftwaffe*'s main-force night offensive against Britain was now in full swing. Six squadrons of Bristol Blenheims, converted to carry airborne radar, did not provide a solution to the night defence problem; they were too slow, the equipment was very unreliable, and its operators lacked experience. A solution was on the horizon in the shape of the fast, heavily armed Bristol Beaufighter, which was just entering service; but this aircraft was beset by more than the usual crop of teething troubles. In November and December 1940, Beaufighters and radar-equipped Blenheims flew over 600 sorties, made seventy-one radar contacts, and succeeded in destroying only four enemy aircraft.

In September 1940, Air Chief Marshal Sir Hugh Dowding, the AOC-in-C Fighter Command, had been ordered by the Air Council to allocate three squadrons of Hawker Hurricanes to night defence, this decision having been taken following the creation of a high-level Night Air Defence Committee earlier in the month. Added to these were three squadrons of Boulton-Paul Defiants, aircraft which, armed solely with a four-gun power-operated turret, had suffered appalling losses in the day-fighter role during the Battle of Britain. During the closing weeks of 1940, these six squadrons of single-engined fighters flew 491 sorties on forty-six nights and destroyed eleven enemy bombers.

In December 1940 No. 4 Operational Training Unit – later renamed No. 54 OTU – was established at Church Fenton to train night fighter crews. It may be that *Luftwaffe* Intelligence got wind of the OTU's activities, because on the night of 15 January 1941 the station was attacked by an intruding Junkers 88 of NJG 2, which badly damaged two Defiants and a Blenheim. Earlier in the month, another intruder had also attacked and badly damaged a No. 10 Squadron Whitley near Catterick. On the night of 10 February 1941 the intruders threw their weight against the Lincolnshire airfields of No. 5 Group, destroying seven aircraft returning from raids on Germany and Holland. Despite encounters with RAF night-fighters, all the intruders – nine aircraft – returned to base.

Delays in the production of AI Mk IV airborne radar meant that the planned target of five Beaufighter squadrons would not be reached before the spring of 1941, and in the meantime it was the Blenheims, Defiants and Hurricanes that continued to hold the line. In the north, one Defiant squadron, No. 141, was based at Ayr from the end of April 1941, and – with detachments at Acklington – found itself in the middle of the May Blitz on Clydeside and Tyneside, its crews claiming eight victories. Although still not radar-equipped, the Defiant was proving itself unexpectedly suited to the night-fighter role; experience had taught crews that if the pilot could manoeuvre his aircraft to a position beneath an enemy bomber, the gunner, elevating his guns at an angle, could usually inflict punishing damage on it. It was a technique developed further by the *Luftwaffe*'s night-fighter force later in the war, when aircraft fitted with upwards-firing guns inflicted severe losses on the RAF's heavy bombers.

March 1941 was a significant month, for it saw the operational debut of ground controlled interception (GCI) stations such as that at Patrington, on the Humber estuary. This, together with the conversion of five of Fighter Command's six Blenheim squadrons to Beaufighters, brought about a dramatic change in the Command's fortunes just in time to counter the *Luftwaffe*'s Blitz on London, Merseyside, Tyneside, Clydeside and other targets. The Hurricane and Defiant squadrons allocated to night defence also added to this change as a result of their increased experience, and because they too derived assistance from GCI. Hitherto, sector controllers had been able to bring night-fighter crews to within about 5 miles (8 km) of a target, and since the range of AI Mk IV was only about 3 miles (5 km), it still needed a fair slice of luck to make a successful interception. The much more precise information provided by the GCI stations made the task far easier, and matters improved still further with the introduction of AI Mk VII, which had a 7 mile (11 km) range and a low-level capability. For the first time, the Mk VII, together with information passed on by the Chain Home Low radar stations – the low-level part of the general warning system – gave night fighter crews the ability to intercept low-flying minelayers and reconnaissance aircraft which had been operating off the British east coast almost with impunity.

The figures themselves speak for the general improvement in the overall air defence system by the summer of 1941. In February the enemy lost only four aircraft to fighters and eight to AA, but during March night fighters shot down twenty-two enemy bombers and the AA guns seventeen. In April the score rose to forty-eight for the fighters and thirty-nine for the guns, and in the first two weeks of

May the loss rate assumed serious proportions, ninety-six bombers being shot down by fighters and thirty-two by AA guns. In addition, ten others were lost due to unknown causes.

Following a final spate of intense attacks on London, the Midlands and Merseyside, the *Luftwaffe*'s spring Blitz on Britain gradually petered out at the end of May 1941 as the Germans transferred the bulk of their bomber force to the east in readiness for Operation Barbarossa, the invasion of Russia, or to the Balkans. Although bombing attacks continued on a sporadic basis during 1941, these tended to follow intruder-type tactics, only small numbers of aircraft being involved. As for the dedicated intruder squadrons, these continued to concentrate on the bomber bases of Lincolnshire and East Anglia in the spring of 1941, and forays into northern airspace were few. Nevertheless, they did occur, and on the night of 16/17 April a Ju 88 flown by *Feldwebel* Wilhelm Breetz, one of NJG 2's most experienced pilots, fell victim to the Tyne AA defences. Another experienced intruder pilot, *Leutnant* Heinz Volker, had better luck in the early hours of 26 April, destroying a Blenheim and a Defiant at Church Fenton and damaging two more aircraft in a combined bombing and strafing attack. Volker also claimed two more aircraft destroyed that night in attacks on the Lincolnshire airfields.

Intruder attacks continued during June and were again directed against Lincolnshire and East Anglia, but on the night of the 13th the intruders suffered a severe setback when three Junkers 88s failed to return, all falling victim to the Beaufighters of No. 25 Squadron from Wittering. This was not, however, by any means the beginning of the end for the intruders; Beaufighters accounted for only three more before the middle of October, although others fell to AA fire and, in one case, to a Douglas Havoc night fighter of No. 85 Squadron. What did spell the end of intruder operations over England was a personal instruction from Adolf Hitler on 13 October 1941, ordering them to cease. The reason was purely one of propaganda. With the RAF's night-bombing effort steadily increasing, Hitler wanted the German people to see the 'terror bombers' destroyed over the Reich territory; faraway victories over England did nothing to improve their morale. For General Kammhuber, commanding Germany's night defences, it was a bitter blow; what was potentially his most potent weapon had been struck from his hand, and no argument would sway the *Führer*.

What, then, had the intruder force – which never numbered more than twenty or thirty serviceable aircraft – achieved in just over a year of operations? It had certainly destroyed over fifty aircraft over England, together with an estimated thirty more over the North Sea. About forty others sustained damage as a consequence of intruder attacks. The cost to the Germans was twenty-seven aircraft, plus seven more destroyed in accidents. After many pitfalls, as we have seen, the RAF's night fighter defences were at last becoming organized. Thanks to improved GCI techniques and better radar, the night defences enjoyed increasing success. During the so-called Baedecker raids of 1942, when the *Luftwaffe* attacked targets of historic or cultural importance, night fighters accounted for most of the sixty-seven enemy bombers destroyed, mostly Dornier 217s of KG 2, between April and July.

Meanwhile, the RAF was stepping up its intruder missions over occupied Europe, using a mixture of Hawker Hurricanes, Boulton Paul Defiants, Bristol Blenheims and Douglas Havocs. One particularly successful Hurricane intruder pilot was Flight

The cannon-armed Hawker Hurricane Mk II was a principal RAF night-intruder type in 1941–2. (Author's collection)

Lieutenant Richard Stevens, who began his combat career with No. 151 Squadron at RAF Manston. A former civil pilot who had flown the cross-Channel mail route at night and in all weathers, Stevens was thirty years old and a very experienced man by the time he joined No. 151 Squadron at the tail-end of the Battle of Britain, in October 1940. At this time the Germans had switched most of their effort to night attacks, and night after night Stevens watched in frustration as the German bombers droned overhead towards the red glare of burning London. He constantly sought permission to try his hand at intercepting the raiders, and at last, one night in December, it was granted.

His early night patrols were disappointing. For several nights running, although the Manston controller assured him that the sky was stiff with enemy bombers, Stevens saw nothing. Then, on the night of 15 January 1941, the shellbursts of the London AA defences led him to a Dornier 17 of 4/KG3, which he chased up to 30,000 ft (9,000 metres) and then almost down to ground level as the German pilot tried to shake him off. But Stevens hung on, and after two or three short bursts the bomber went down and exploded on the ground. It was No. 151 Squadron's first night victory, and there were more to come. On a second patrol that night, Stevens caught a Heinkel 111 of 2/KG 53 at 17,000 ft (5,000 metres), heading for London, and shot it down into the Thames estuary. Three of the four crew members baled out and were captured. The night's work earned Stevens a Distinguished Flying Cross.

Shortly after the award of his DFC, he developed ear trouble and was grounded for a while, but he celebrated his return to action on 8 April 1941 by shooting down two Heinkel 111s in one night. Two nights later he got another Heinkel and a Junkers 88, and a few days later he received a Bar to his DFC. He destroyed yet another Heinkel on the 19th, and on 7 May he accounted for two more. Three nights after that, his claim was one Heinkel destroyed and one probably destroyed. He shot down a further Heinkel on 13 June, damaged one on the 22nd, and on 3 July sent a Junkers 88 down in flames. There seemed to be no end to his success; at this time he was the RAF's top-scoring night fighter pilot, enjoying a considerable lead over men who flew the radar-equipped Beaufighters.

Stevens experienced a lot of frustration during the summer months of 1941. In June the Germans invaded the Soviet Union, and by the end of July they had withdrawn many of their bomber units from the Western Front. Raids at night over Britain became fewer, and although Stevens continued to fly his lone patrols, for weeks he never saw an enemy bomber. Then, one evening in October, he spotted a Junkers 88 slipping inland over the coast of East Anglia and attacked it. The Junkers jettisoned its bombs and turned away, diving low over the water, but Stevens caught it with a burst of fire and sent it into the sea. It was his fourteenth victory. Soon afterwards, he was posted to another Hurricane unit, No. 253 Squadron, as a flight commander, and he immediately set about devising a plan to take the war to the enemy by flying night-intruder operations over the German airfields in Holland and Belgium. He flew his first on the night of 12/13 December, the day when it was announced that he had been awarded the Distinguished Service Order. He loitered in the vicinity of the bomber airfield at Gilze-Rijn, in Holland, but saw no aircraft and returned home in disappointment. Three nights later he took off again, heading for the same destination, and never returned. The signal that his squadron commander sent to Group HQ was simple and concise. 'One Hurricane IIC (long range), 253 Squadron, took off Manston 19.40 hours, 15.12.41, to go to Gilze. It has failed to return and is beyond maximum endurance.' Somewhere out there over darkened Europe, or more probably over the waters of the Channel, Richard Stevens,who had fought a lonely, single-handed battle in the night sky for over a year, had met an equally lonely fate.

The majority of the home-based Hurricane II squadrons took part in night intruder operations at one time or another during 1942, and some became specialists in the role. No. 1 Squadron, for example, which was based at RAF Tangmere, destroyed twenty-two enemy aircraft over occupied Europe between 1 April and 1 July that year before moving to Northumberland to convert to Typhoon fighter-bombers, and no fewer than fifteen of these victories were gained by one pilot, Flight Lieutenant Karel Kuttelwascher. A highly competent and experienced pilot, Kuttelwascher – known by the simpler abbreviation of 'Kut' to his squadron colleagues – had flown with the Czech air force for four years before his country was overrun by the Germans, after which he had made his way to Britain via France. He scored his first three kills – all Messerschmitt 109s – while flying convoy protection and bomber escort missions over the Channel in the spring and early summer of 1941, but it was when No. 1 Squadron went over to night intruder operations in April 1942 that Kut really got into his stride. In April 1942 he destroyed three Junkers 88s, three Dornier 217s and a Heinkel 111, and on the night of 4/5 May he shot down three

Czech Flight Lieutenant Karel Kuttelwascher was a highly experienced pilot, and a successful intruder. (Author's collection)

Heinkel 111s over St André. He destroyed a Dornier 217 off Dunkirk on 2/3 June, and on the following night he visited St André again to destroy a Heinkel 111 and a Dornier 217, as well as damaging another Dornier.

St André was once again the target on 21/22 June, when Kut shot down a Junkers 88 and damaged another. A Dornier 217 went down before his guns near Trevières on 29/29 June, and his last two victims, also Dornier 217s, were brought down near Dinard on the night of 1/2 July, when he also damaged a third Dornier. That brought Kut's score to eighteen destroyed, with one probable (a Messerschmitt 109, his first combat in the RAF, on 2 February 1941) and five damaged. In addition, he may have claimed up to six victories while flying Morane 406 fighters in the Battle of France. After the war, he became a captain with British European Airways, flying Vikings and Elizabethans. He died of a heart attack on 17 August 1959, at the untimely age of 42.

No. 1 Squadron's other leading scorer in the summer of 1942 was the squadron commander, Squadron Leader James MacLachlan, but with five enemy bombers destroyed and three damaged, he was a long way behind his Czech colleague. A remarkable character, 'Mac' had scored six victories in the Battle of Britain and two more over Malta, but had himself been shot down and badly wounded in February 1941, losing his left arm above the elbow. He took command of No. 1 Squadron in November 1941, having been fitted with an artificial arm in the meantime.

The year 1942 saw the debut of the night fighter that really tipped the scales: the de Havilland Mosquito. In October No. 25 Squadron became the north's first Mosquito night fighter squadron, moving to Church Fenton and displacing No. 54 OTU, which went to Charterhall on the Scottish Borders. Later in the month No. 410 Squadron also re-equipped at Acklington. The advent of the Mosquito was timely, for KG 2's fast Dornier 217s, which were capable of 300 mph (480 kph) at low altitude, were causing problems for the defences. And it was not only historic towns that were hit; Middlesbrough, for example, after a break of five months, was attacked four times between the middle of April and the end of July 1942. It is also worth recording that, outside the great conurbations of London and Merseyside, the hardest-hit city in Britain was Hull. By the war's end, only 6,000 out of 93,000 buildings in Hull had escaped bomb damage, most of it incurred during three major attacks in March and May 1941. Because of its geographical location, Hull was an easy target. It was heavily attacked twice during Operation Steinbock, the so-called Little Blitz of January to May 1944, conducted by all available German bombers on the Western Front. During these two attacks, carried out by Junkers 88s, Dornier 217s and Heinkel 177s, 25 Squadron (Coltishall), 264 Squadron (Church Fenton) and 307 Polish Squadron (Drem) claimed eleven enemy aircraft between them. As a matter of note, the Little Blitz cost the *Luftwaffe* 329 aircraft, of which 129 were destroyed by Mosquitoes equipped with Mk VIII AI radar.

By the beginning of 1943 the RAF's night fighter squadrons were turning increasingly from defence to offence, and it was the

The Dornier 217's relatively high speed made it a suitable aircraft for fast intruder hit-and-run operations. (Author's collection)

Mosquito that spearheaded the intruder offensive. The Mosquito's long range and heavy armament of four 20 mm cannon made it highly suitable for the night-intruder role, as well as for local night air defence. The intruder Mosquitoes (and Beaufighters), although stripped of their AI for operations over enemy territory, were fitted with a device named Serrate which, developed by the Telecommunications Research Establishment as a result of information on enemy night-fighting radars brought back by special countermeasures aircraft, enabled the British fighters to home in to the enemy's airborne radar transmissions. It had a range of about 50 miles (80 km), and was first used operationally in June 1943 by No. 141 Squadron, which scored twenty-three kills in three months with its help. No. 141 Squadron's commander was Wing Commander J.R.D. 'Bob' Braham, whose combat report describes a night action off the Dutch island of Ameland on the night of 17/18 August 1943. Braham was flying a Beaufighter Mk VI, and his navigator was Flight Lieutenant H. Jacobs.

We took off from Coltishall at 2200 hours on intruder patrol to Stade. We flew to a point north of Schiermonnikoog and then turned NE at 2254. We continued on course for about five minutes when we sighted one Me 110 flying east and jinking. We turned and followed him towards the coast, closing in on the aircraft until we were at 300 yards range, 20 degrees starboard astern and a little below. Fire was opened with a two-second burst from all guns and strikes were seen all over the enemy aircraft. Smoke came from the port engine and the Me 110 dived to port. We gave him another two-second burst from 250 yards and he caught fire and dived into the sea, burning on the water. Immediately afterwards we saw a second Me 110 (which had been chasing us) a little above and turning gently to starboard on an easterly course. We gave a one-second burst of cannon and machine gun at 50 yards in a gentle turn. The enemy aircraft appeared to blow up and we had to pull up and turn to port to avoid ramming it. At that point we saw one man bale out and his parachute open, and the enemy aircraft dived vertically into the sea in flames ... we landed at Wittering at 0145.

Towards the end of 1944, Mosquitoes equipped with the latest AI radar were cleared to operate over enemy territory, and the old Serrate Mk I was replaced by a new version, the Mk IV. Some aircraft were also equipped with a new device known as Perfectos, which emitted a pulse that triggered the IFF (identification friend/foe) sets of German night fighters and enabled the

Mosquitoes to home on to the answering signal. Nevertheless, No. 100 Group's fighter force never really succeeded in getting to grips with the enemy night fighters. Quite apart from equipment problems, the Mosquito crews were faced with the formidable task of operating deep inside enemy territory as complete freelancers, with no help from other quarters. Furthermore, enemy fighters had to be intercepted before they entered the bomber stream, because once they were inside the stream it was extremely difficult to make radar contact with them owing to the profusion of other echoes. The tactics employed by the Mosquitoes usually began with a bombing and cannon attack on enemy night-fighter airfields a few minutes before the bomber stream entered the area of German GCI radar coverage. Other Mosquitoes would work on the flanks of the stream, about 40 miles (65 km) from it and at a higher altitude, in the hope of intercepting enemy fighters before they reached the bombers. As the bombers were on their way home from the target, more Mosquito fighter-bombers loitered in the vicinity of the German airfields, waiting to catch the night fighters as they came in to land.

One Mosquito night fighter/intruder team that enjoyed considerable success was Flight Lieutenant James Benson and Squadron Leader Lewis Brandon (navigator) of No. 157 Squadron. Together, they scored seven confirmed kills, with a number of claims for aircraft probably destroyed and damaged, and also destroyed six V-1 flying bombs in the summer of 1944. On the night of 11/12 September 1944, while flying bomber-support operations with No. 100 Group, they were flying over the island of Seeland, off the south-east coast of Denmark, when Brandon picked up a transmission from an enemy night fighter radar. A few moments later, he made contact with the suspect aircraft and steered Benson towards it.

In the clear moonlight, the enemy was identified as a Junkers 188; it was flying in broad circles, apparently orbiting a German radio beacon. Benson slid in astern of the 188 and fired a burst into it, seeing his 20 mm shells strike home on the night fighter's starboard wing root. The 188 lost speed rapidly, its starboard engine catching fire, and Benson had to pull up sharply to avoid a collision. The 188 was last seen plunging earthwards, streaming flames. At that moment, Brandon picked up another contact. It was a second Ju 188, and it had probably been engaged in a night-fighting exercise with the first. Benson closed in rapidly and gave the Junkers a two-second burst; bright flames streamed back from the enemy's ruptured fuel tanks and it dropped away towards the Danish coast, shedding great chunks of wreckage. The Mosquito sped through the cloud of smoke and debris that the Junkers left in its wake; when Benson and Brandon returned to base they found their aircraft smothered in oil and scarred by pieces of flying metal.

In 1943–4 the *Luftwaffe* once again mounted frequent intruder operations, using mainly Me 410 and Ju 188 aircraft. We can see a measure of what they might have achieved, had these aircraft been committed in greater numbers, in one attack on American air bases in East Norfolk on 2 April 1944, when intruders destroyed thirteen B-24 Liberators and, in the panic, two more were shot down by their own airfield defences.

On the night of 3–4 March 1945, at the eleventh hour, the *Luftwaffe* launched Operation Gisela, sending 140 intruders over England. They attacked fourteen bomber bases and destroyed nineteen bombers on airfields north and south of the Humber. A smaller follow-on raid was attempted on the next night, the two attacks costing the *Luftwaffe* around twenty aircraft. In the second raid, a Junkers Ju 88G-6 of 13/NJG 3 was shot down at 01.51 at Sutton-on-Derwent during an attack on Elvington. It was the last German aircraft to be brought down on British soil.

Index

Page numbers in *italics* refer to illustrations.